WORLD WAR II
WAC

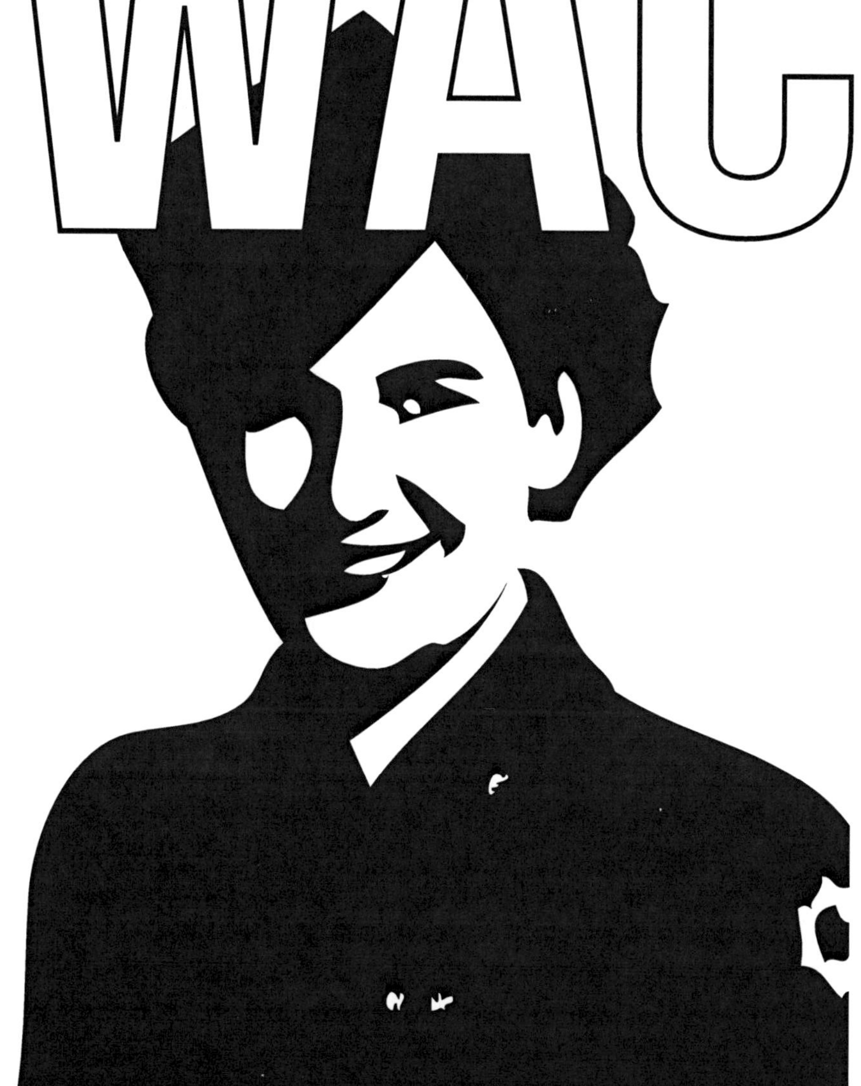

WORLD WAR II
WAC

HELEN DENTON

as told to ROBERT O. BABCOCK

Bob Babcock

DeedsPublishing
Marietta, GA

Published by Deeds Publishing
Marietta, GA
www.deedspublishing.com

Printed in the United States of America

Cover design by Mark Babcock

Library of Congress Cataloging-in-Publications Data is available upon request.

ISBN: 978-1-937565-46-6

Books are available in quantity for promotional or premium use. For information, write Deeds Publishing, PO Box 682212, Marietta, GA 30068 or info@deedspublishing.com.

First Edition, 2012

10 9 8 7 6 5 4 3 2 1

DEDICATION

I am dedicating this book to a very dear friend, Patricia Swords, who for over forty years has been beside me through good times and sad times. She has been my faithful friend. We met in 1969 when she traveled to Atlanta with her mother to find a job. She had just graduated from high school. We encountered her at church that Sunday and she indicated she wanted to find a job. I recommended she apply at Delta Air Lines. The next week I looked up from my desk and saw her walking down the hall. During my last years at Delta, we worked side by side and we have been that close ever since. For forty some years she has been my friend. We have had happy and exciting times as well as sad times, since both of us have lost our husbands. I'm proud to call her my friend.

CONTENTS

50% of the profits of this book will benefit
USO Georgia, Inc.

INTRODUCTION

For fifty years, Helen Denton didn't tell a soul, not even her husband or son, about the significant role she played in the historic invasion of France in World War II—Operation Overlord, or D-Day, as it is commonly called. The officers had told her, "Do not talk about what you are doing" and Helen dutifully followed those orders for all those years. She remembers, "I never asked any of the girls (that I was living and working with) what they were working on, and they never asked me."

Assigned to the communications department of General Eisenhower's headquarters in England in early 1944, Helen took dictation from American, British, Canadian, and Australian officers. She sat at her Royal manual typewriter in an 8-by-10-foot room and recorded page after page of orders—shipping schedules, flight plans, troop movements, and thousands of other details that had to be included in the detailed orders. No typos allowed. Everything she worked on was stamped TOP SECRET. The name of the project was OVERLORD. She was the WAC (Women's Army Corps) who typed the orders for D-Day, and later had the honor of personally handing the finished document to General Eisenhower.

Less than two months after the invasion, Helen found herself on one of the Normandy, France beaches she had typed in those secret orders—and it was there, on her first morning in France, that she met a young sergeant from Georgia, Staff Sergeant Noel Denton. Little did she know that morning that he would later become her husband.

Read on to learn the details of this amazing woman's experiences in World War II, and since she returned home. In addition to the history she helped make in England, Utah Beach, and Paris in WWII, her extremely active life in retirement can be an inspiration to the generation of Baby Boomers and others who are facing their own retirement years.

FOREWORD

After my retirement from IBM in 2002, I formed a non-profit organization, Americans Remembered, and became an official founding partner of the Veterans History Project, part of the Library of Congress. The VHP's mission is to preserve memories of America's veterans and home front workers from all our nation's wars.

Always looking for veterans to interview, I was introduced by Colonel (Retired) Jim Stapleton, a fellow vet I had served with in Vietnam, to Helen Denton early in 2003.

My wife, Jan, and I were awed by the story Helen told us. She inspired us to continue to preserve more stories of many more veterans of all our nation's wars.

Over the next few years, I would call on Helen to help me with Veterans History Project work, speaking to groups who needed to hear her story and to tell their own. We both were asked to participate with the VHP in the dedication of the World War II Monument in Washington, DC in May 2004. I often told others about Helen Kogel Denton, her unique place in American history, and her ongoing enthusiasm about telling her story to others of all ages.

After several years of no contact, I again saw Helen, in April 2012, at the monthly Atlanta Vietnam Veterans Business Association meeting, where she was our speaker. Sitting at lunch before her speech, I asked her, "Helen, why haven't you put your story into a book?"

She responded with, "I've often thought about it but don't really know how to even start."

Helen was unaware that I was the founder of Deeds Publishing, a small publishing business where my family and I are busy publishing books for many first time authors. My response was, "I know how—when do we start?" Just that quickly, we shook hands and formed a partnership to write and publish this book.

After Helen's talk about her experiences working on General Eisenhower's staff in WWII, I stood up in front of our group and told them, "Helen will be back here around Veterans Day of this year to sign the book that she and I are going to write." And, as the saying goes, the rest is history. Read on to learn about this great woman's life as an American patriot.

-Bob Babcock, co-author, October, 2012

Helen Kogel Denton's Veterans History Project interview can be viewed online at:
http://lcweb2.loc.gov/diglib/vhp/story/loc.natlib.afc2001001.04639/video?ID=mv0001001

GROWING UP IN SOUTH DAKOTA

To best understand Helen's story, you need to go back to the latter part of the 1800's. In her own words, she describes her family background that established the values that have directed the rest of her life.

My grandparents lived in Iowa but worked for another farmer. When the Dakota Territory was opened for homesteaders, my grandfather decided to load up his sons to find some land. He settled on 640 acres of land near what is now Lane, South Dakota where they built a one-room house from prairie sod. The homestead law dictated that a person must reside on the land, continuously, for five years before one would be the full owner. In order to fulfill the requirement, my grandfather left behind one son while he went back to Iowa to retrieve the rest of his family. That son was my father.

So, at the age of 12 years old, this young man was left to face the upcoming winter of Dakota Territory with grandfather and the rest of the family in Iowa. There wasn't any choice as a covered wagon could not make a lengthy trip like that in one season. Grandfather left some provisions (but not much) and a violin. All other provisions were acquired from hunting and fishing.

Being alone on the prairie—and I mean really alone—would, and did, drive some men over the edge. But this young man, Phillip, had strength, and a violin. It was during this time that he taught himself how to play. I imagine it was probably a good thing that he was alone so no one could hear him.

Well, nearly no one. Each time Phillip would play his violin, he noticed a lone Indian on his horse at the top of the hill about a quarter of a mile away. They never spoke to each other, or even waved, but that Indian would always come. When Phillip quit playing, the Indian would turn his horse around and leave. On many mornings, Phillip would find fresh meat, and even firewood, outside his prairie sod house—the Indians were looking out for him and taking care of him.

Of course, as luck would have it, the worst blizzard in the history of the Territory came one month earlier than expected. This caught the inexperienced Phillip without provisions. As the blizzard wore on for days and days, he was getting hungry. Water was made from snow. He would crack open the door, scoop some snow into a cup, melt it, and then have a drink.

By the time the blizzard ended, he was so weak he wasn't sure he had the energy to shoot a rabbit, let alone skin it and cook it. But, he had to try. As he shouldered open the door with all the snow piled up against it, he noticed something unusual. Blood. Blood? He pushed further and there, lying on top of the fresh snow, was a freshly killed deer from his Indian 'friend.' That Indian, whoever he was, saved Phillip's life. And, of course, if it weren't for a benevolent Indian, I wouldn't be here to write this story. The actions of one person did so much for the future.

It was from this man, Phillip, and the woman he married, who also came to Dakota Territory via covered wagon, that my family has its roots. My father had these values all through his life: don't give up, take responsibility, be benevolent, work hard and fair—and, most importantly, give thanks to God. He passed those values down to all of his children, including me.

Soon after the spring thaw, my grandfather arrived with the rest of the family and all the supplies and provisions they could bring with them. Work began immediately, with everyone pitching in. A real wooden two-story house was constructed, a large barn, chicken house, hog house, and other assorted buildings sprung up. Farming started that spring, with plowing accomplished by three teams of beautiful Morgan horses. All harnesses, bits, and reins were kept in perfect order and the Morgans were washed down each evening and put into clean stalls. After all, if it wasn't for these wonderful animals, farming would be impossible.

Our family grew after my parents were married, with six boys and three girls making up the typically large farmer's family. I was born on

December 9, 1921, the next to youngest child in our family. We all had our chores and hardships, but thought nothing of it since that was the way it was in those days.

The conveniences that we enjoy today and take for granted were luxuries then—such things as indoor running water and electricity. My father was ingenious for his time and we had the first electric lights in that part of the country. Batteries were available by this time so my father built a small power plant in the barn. He had a small gasoline engine with an alternator attached to it. From the alternator, a charge was sent to a series of 32-volt batteries on the shelf. From these batteries, a wire was strung from the barn to the house. It was this power that my mother used for her washing machine and that my father used for the cream separator and lights in the barn. It was my brothers' responsibility to keep the batteries filled with distilled water. Whenever we needed the electricity, we primed the little engine, and voila—we had electricity. Our farm was considered MOST modern and was the envy of all around. Even so, farming was hard and took long days of work year around.

I always thought we were well off. We had plenty of food, were all healthy, and we had a loving family relationship, centered around our strong faith in God. Everyone had chores to do before the bus picked us up for school. When I started school in the first grade all but my oldest brother were attending. We seldom missed a day of school, unless we were too sick to attend.

Living on the farm provided us with plenty of meat and vegetables from the garden. My mother made all of our clothes, often using flour sacks with the colorful designs printed on the cloth. In those days, flour manufacturers made their sacks decorative for that purpose. Many, many families in the Midwest used these sacks for everything from dresses to table cloths, so it was quite common and not out of place at all.

We rode to school in buses until the roads became impassable due to snow or mud, then we traveled in a sled or wagon. If it was cold, my mother would heat a brick in the oven and wrap us in blankets and we always made it. My first year in school, 1926, we had one of the worst blizzards and all seven of us children had to stay in town with any citizen who would take us in. It was two days before my father could come in with a sled and pick us up.

Our evenings were spent making sure our homework was finished; then we gathered together in the living room. My dad would play the violin or accordion, and Hazel and I would sing duets. Hazel learned how to play the piano and was very talented. Later in life she took piano lessons and both of us had singing lessons. We often sang at community programs and in school. The family often sat at the dining room table and played the card game Hearts. The table would seat twelve and was always ready for use.

Holidays were very special, with a goose for Thanksgiving and turkey for Christmas and New Year. We made lots of homemade candy. Presents were always clothes or something useful. Once we had a Christmas tree but we had to use candles and found out that wasn't practical. We sometimes got hand-me-down clothes from a cousin—it was like Christmas when that box arrived. We were thrilled to death and very grateful.

We were all well-loved with that many children. My mother and father often had one night a month, weather permitting, when they went square dancing at the Community Hall in Woonsocket. We had a movie house in Lane, the nearest town. They often played Roy Rogers or Lone Ranger movies for 10 cents. Saturday evening was the only time we all went to town.

Family gatherings were often our best time. We had a touring car that had two pull-down seats attached to the back of the front seats. The back seat would seat four, my dad put a board over the pull down seats to seat three more, and three would sit in the front seat if necessary. We always made Mass on Sunday or any other time. Later, my father bought a Model A for my older brothers to use. Life was very good for all of us.

Feeding a family this size was an ongoing operation. We butchered our own beef and pork so we always had meat. Our garden was huge so we canned everything we needed. Dad bought flour and sugar in 50 pound bags to see us through the winter months. Of course we had eggs, chickens, all types of poultry. We had a cellar under the house, which was our storage area, especially in the summer time, as well as a storm area for the tornadoes.

In 1929, the stock market crashed, the banks closed and everyone was in a panic—the Great Depression had begun. While bankers were jumping out of windows to their death in large cities across America, South Dakota had more serious problems—we were experiencing a terrible drought. No crops would grow because of the lack of rain. The drought caused dust storms that would block out the sun and pile dust over fences and fence posts like snow. Whenever we saw one coming, everyone soaked towels and placed them around the windows and doors to try to keep the dust out. It did help, but not much.

Dust was everywhere—on the tables, floors, curtains, furniture… you could even taste it in your food. Some dust storms were so bad you didn't see the sun for days. And tumble weeds… the big, round, dry, brown, leafless weeds that would blow across the prairies were everywhere. Some were four feet in diameter and plugged up doorways, fence lines, and anything the dust didn't get into. On the good side, we kids would use the tumbleweeds as sails and would sit in our little wagon and hold up one of these weeds to propel us down the road.

As though that wasn't enough, when there is a drought, grasshoppers appear the next year—millions and millions of grasshoppers. They can strip a field of wheat or corn in hours as they move from field to field. Any vegetation is eaten or destroyed, including grass, hay, or alfalfa. So the next year there weren't any crops, either. Nonetheless, we counted our blessings because we lived on a farm that gave us meat, potatoes, and some vegetables for our family. We weren't going to starve.

In order to support the family, my father decided to hold barn dances in our hay loft. We had a very large barn and by decorating it with tree branches and polishing the floor, it made a very rustic dance pavilion. On Friday night we held square dances and on Saturday night were the modern dances. Every one of our family pitched in to clean the yards, put machinery away, clean out the barn, fill rain barrels with water for fire prevention to get ready for the weekend dances. My mother would bake hot dog buns to sell during intermission, along with Nehi soft drinks. My youngest brother and I could stay up until it was time for my mother to go back to the house to cook the hot dogs—then it was time for us to retire.

Later on, three of my brothers left home to find jobs harvesting crops in Minnesota and Iowa. It took until 1940 before our farm land once again produced crops. By then, the draft for military service had started and two of my brothers were called up.

I graduated from high school in June, 1939 and had decided I wanted to go to college. Knowing I had to pay my own way, I worked from July, 1939 to September, 1940 in a grocery store and left for Mankato, Minnesota in September, 1940 for the fall term in a business school, which gave us good training in typing and bookkeeping. I lived with a family and helped with household duties for my room and board, and walked to school. On weekends, my brother, who was married and lived in Winnebago, would pick me up to spend a couple of days with them.

Over the summer months of 1941, I came home and had a job in a grocery store in Woonsocket, saving every penny. I went back to Mankato for a second year, and still worked in a private home for my room and board.

On December 7, 1941, a Sunday morning, I had been in church and was just entering our house when I realized something terrible had happened. The family was sitting around the radio and I could hear the announcer talking about the bombing of Pearl Harbor. By this time, Clement and Jerome had been called up for the Army. My father was on the Draft Board in our county. They were both serving in the infantry somewhere and I immediately thought about them. We had studied about the terrible problems in Germany my last year in high school, so we were prepared for something—but not the attack in Hawaii and not such devastation. It became personal when I heard that one of our classmates was on the USS Arizona battleship that had been sunk. Everyone was glued to the radio to hear the latest news.

I graduated in June, 1942. I was employed as a bookkeeper in Winnebago by Interstate Power Company for six months and then was transferred to Sherburn, Minnesota, about 25 miles from the main office where I served as Chief Clerk in the office, handling customers, payroll, and secretary to the general manager. I had a room in a private home, but ate my meals in the restaurant.

I was very active in the community. Sherburn was a small town with lots of activity. I was on a bowling team, and of course, attended dances out at the pavilion. I had lots of friends and enjoyed my job. With the war increasing, more and more boys were leaving, and it left a shortage of friends.

In the store window, I had begun to collect pictures of the men who were serving in the military and displaying them for everyone to see who had left. It became quite a collection.

My life appeared like it was on a typical course for a young lady in those days, and then everything changed. I went into the Army…

Helen's brothers were pheasant hunters.

LEFT: Vera Sheal and Helen Kogel – High School graduation 1939
RIGHT: Helen's parents – Philip and Mary Kogel

Helen's brothers – Jerry, Clem, Cecil, Leland (Buck), Everet, and Gordon

The Kogel Family farm in South Dakota

STATESIDE ARMY DUTY

During this time the war was escalating. Every week a busload of young men would leave for the service, leaving fewer and fewer around for us girls to date. One day, a girl friend said, "Let's do something other than just sit at home and watch these men leave." She asked me to accompany her to Minneapolis so she could join the Women's Auxiliary Army Corps (WAAC). I hesitated at first, because I enjoyed my job and was dating a nice man, but I went.

Instead of waiting for her to take her test, I thought I'd like to see what the test was like, and took the examination, thinking I didn't need to accept it. Not realizing that the test was going to be picked up and graded, I passed—and she didn't. When I told the recruiter that I had a job and couldn't leave, she said it was too late, that I had better turn in my resignation; that I would receive a letter with authorization to leave. Two weeks later, I received my summons to report to Fort Des Moines, Iowa for induction. It was difficult to have to call my parents and tell them one more of their children was joining the Army. I asked if they would use some of their rationed gasoline to come over and pick up my clothes, and we could say goodbye. Of course, they did.

An article in the local newspaper announced Helen's enlistment as follows:

Helen Kogel Reports for Duty March 23

Mrs. Harold Gibbons, local WAAC recruiting officer, announces the acceptance of Miss Helen Kogel into that organization on February 27 (1943). Miss Kogel has leave until March 23 when she will report for training at Fort Des Moines.

During her stay in Sherburn, Miss Kogel has been very active in war activities, such as aiding in preparing Christmas packages for the service men, spending a great amount of time in caring for and arranging the fine picture display of service men in the Interstate Power office window, as well as other matters important to the war effort. She is to be sincerely congratulated for this last and greatest step of all in doing her part in war work. Especially is this true when it is considered that she leaves a lucrative secretarial position with the Interstate Power Company.

For any girl wishing to join an auxiliary unit of the military service, Mrs. Gibbons has a complete list of clothes and accessories furnished by the government, as well as a list of practical articles that each girl should provide herself with.

The following newspaper article explains the expanding need for women in military service:

150,000 Recruits Wanted for WAAC

The following communication has been sent to Mrs. Harold Gibbons, WAAC assistant, from the War Department, Washington, D.C. which states the facts as well as they can be stated. It is believed that patriotic women who desire to give as much as they receive will give serious consideration to the whole of this communication. A moment's consideration on their part of the difference between the position of women in the United States and their position under Axis rule should cause them to desire to do everything in their power to establish our system throughout the world.

On November 20, 1942, President Roosevelt authorized the Women's Auxiliary Army Corps to recruit to the strength of 150 thousand—six times its originally intended size. The WAAC wants 75,000 members enrolled by March 31, 1943. This simply means: WAAC enrollment must more than double the present weekly rate and be continued until we reach the goal of 150,000 which will relieve that many soldiers for active military service. Our armies overseas are also requesting units of the WAAC to be assigned to duty with their forces, one of which is already in Africa.

Basic training for WAAC's is at one of the following places: First WAAC Training Center, Fort Des Moines, Iowa; Second

WAAC Training Center, Daytona Beach, Florida; Third WAAC Training Center, Fort Oglethorpe, Georgia. The term is five weeks. One week of orientation and four weeks of basic training, which includes military customs and courtesies, Articles of War, military sanitation, first aid, map reading, safeguarding military information, etc. WAAC auxiliaries who demonstrate their capacity for leadership by their performance while in training, are selected to attend the Officers Candidate School. All WAAC officers now come from the ranks.

The WAACS are replacing soldiers in the United States: in the Army Air Forces, Services of Supply, and Ground Forces; Overseas: in England and Africa, a number of WAACs—the vanguard of many more to follow, are already serving in many capacities with our American troops. The only woman present at the Casablanca Conference between President Roosevelt and Prime Minister Churchill and their staffs was Captain Louise Anderson of the WAAC, attached to General Eisenhower's North African Headquarters, who acted as official secretary.

Mrs. Harold Gibbons will answer all questions, provide an application blank, and tell you exactly how to proceed.

RELEASE A SOLDIER FOR ACTIVE COMBAT DUTY—JOIN THE WAAC!

The first six weeks was spent going through the normal routine of any Army service—drilling, calisthenics, classes, and, of course, KP duty. There were several hundred of us women of all ages, learning to get along and trying to understand what was expected of us.

Finished with basic training, I was assigned to recruitment duty and sent to Kansas City, Missouri—recruiting women to join the WAACs. At first, I was on my own, traveling by car or train to small towns, setting up a recruitment office in the local post office, not far from the office where men were being recruited. It was lonely duty. In those days, young women in a small town had very little to do. I stayed in a hotel, ate meals in the hotel or a nearby restaurant, and spent many lonely nights by myself in a hotel room. After several days working in that town, I would move to another one and start the process over again— and live alone in another small town hotel.

Loneliness was not Helen's only challenge, the following newspaper article describes another challenge she faced...

Nobody Wants to Cash Check for WAAC Auxiliary

A WAAC auxiliary assigned to duty in the St. Joseph Army and WAAC recruiting office in the post office building, had plenty of money today but for all practical purposes she might just as well have been flat broke.

The auxiliary had a government check for $150 made payable to herself but she could find no one to cash it for her. Presenting her credentials at one of the largest banks downtown, payment of the check was refused "for lack of identification," in spite of the fact she possessed a note of identification from the lieutenant in charge of her office who had an account at the bank. She also tried the post office window where Marines and sailors, on recruiting duty here, always cash their paychecks. But there she also met with refusal. It seems that her Army credentials, which identified her as an auxiliary in the women's army auxiliary corps assigned to recruiting duty in the post office building, were "not sufficient identification."

When last seen just before noon, she was trying to borrow lunch money and was offering her $150 government check as collateral for a 50-cent loan.

Maybe in response to the situation they reported above, and to help Helen and her fellow WAACs, the St. Joseph, Missouri newspaper printed the following two articles which Helen kept in her scrapbook...

WAAC in Charge
Auxiliary Helen Kogel Takes Over
Army Recruiting Office

Auxiliary Helen Kogel, recently transferred here, now has charge of the Army and WAAC recruiting office, ground floor of the federal building. She succeeded Private Eddie Campbell, who has been transferred to Leavenworth, Kan.

Auxiliary Kogel, whose home was at Woonsocket, S.D., has been in the WAAC since March 1, 1943, and received her basic training at Des Moines, Iowa. She was transferred from the district office in Kansas City.

She also is in charge of the enlistment of Army air cadets. Boys 17 and 18 years old are eligible for enlistment and now are given their examinations at Rosecrans Field here.

TOP O' THE MORNING
By Robert Gordon

We're glad St. Joseph is going to have a contingent of those sincere and patriotic young women of the WAAC stationed at Rosecrans Field. About 155 of the uniformed auxiliaries and their officers are to take over duties at the A. F. T. C. base here and release an equal number of men for other military activities.

We're glad of another thing in connection with the WAACs. They're being taken seriously now, after a period in which they were made the butt of some rather unkind jokes. The reason they're being taken seriously is that they have demonstrated, quite conclusively too, they can perform a lot of military duties just as well or perhaps better than men. They can operate telephones, do clerical work, drive cars and in some places they are flying planes. As a general rule, they are infinitely better on detail work than men. While this has nothing to do with the WAACs, in some war industries, notably in plane assemblies, they have shown unusual dexterity in draftsmanship and the intricate electrical wiring and installations required in big bombers.

The other afternoon we happened to be in the army recruiting office, on the ground floor of the federal building here. This office, by the way, is now in charge of a WAAC, Auxiliary Helen Kogel. While we were there a man sauntered in and asked to see the Army recruiting officer.

"I'm the recruiting officer," Miss Kogel tactfully replied. We didn't wait to see what the man wanted, but from the efficiency with which she was handling Uncle Sam's military affairs in the office, we know his business was well taken care of.

Anyway, we're delighted the WAACs are coming to town. The 300 of them assigned to duty in North Africa have done a splendid job, according to General Eisenhower, and those here will carry on the tradition already established by their corps.

It was in Rosecrans, Missouri that I met Robert Young, the movie star. He had come into town for a bond drive and some publicity. I was asked by the Army base public relations captain to drive the jeep that would pick Mr. Young up at the airport. It was a thrill for me to meet a movie star.

On September 1, 1943, the WAACs were accepted into the Army. We dropped the Auxiliary from WAAC (Women's Auxiliary Army Corps) and became the Women's Army Corps (WAC).

In November of 1943, I was in Big Bend, Kansas when I started having terrible stomach pains. The next morning I went to a doctor and was rushed to the hospital with a ruptured appendix and was operated on. I spent three weeks in the Army Air Corps hospital, the only female patient there, and recovered to return to duty. While in the hospital, I met Max and Buddy Baer, two famous boxers, who went around visiting troops.

A get well letter, written by Helen's commanding officer, follows...

KANSAS RECRUITING DISTRICT
Office of the
Women's Army Corps

Pfc Kogel: "I have a pain in my abdomen."

Army Doctor: "Young lady, Officers have abdomens, Sergeants have stomach aches. You have a belly ache."

Greetings and Salutations!

We'll be thinking of you—in Garden City, Hutch and Wichita!

Some day I'll favor you with some of my *original verse!*

Get well soon—

Love,

Lt. Rowlands

Shortly after my return to duty, I was taken out of recruitment and sent to Fort Crook, in Omaha, Nebraska. My time at Fort Crook was very limited, and quite different from my experiences in recruiting. With several hundred WACs in a regular barracks, living conditions were very different from living in hotels as I had done in recruiting duty. This was more like when I had taken Basic Training at Fort Des Moines, Iowa. My first assignment at Fort Crook was secretary to the post commandant. Working there, I really learned how a post is run. We worked closely with the men, but at chow time we went to our own WAC mess hall. Of course we found plenty of time to associate with the men after duty hours in the recreation area and the canteen. Fort Crook was also a prison for Italian prisoners of war, but we didn't have anything to do with them.

I had to make new friends, which I enjoyed, and living in a barracks made me feel like I was in the real Army. Although short lived, my time at Fort Crook was enjoyable, and another step toward my ultimate role that I never dreamed would happen.

In January 1944, I was taking mail into the post commander's office, ready to take dictation, when he opened a telegram asking him to select one girl from our group for a special assignment. When I asked him what the assignment was, he told me it was an overseas assignment working on the staff of General Eisenhower. I immediately volunteered and he accepted me. It was a case of my being in the right place at the right time. He gave me a five-day pass to go home and then travel to Fort Oglethorpe, in Atlanta, Georgia, for assignment.

Helen's travel and change of station orders read as follows—understanding military abbreviations became very important, and second nature, to those who only months before had been civilians and this type of writing would have been nothing more than gibberish to them:

HEADQUARTERS
Fort Crook, Nebraska

RESTRICTED

SPECIAL ORDERS)   hfh/iem

Number 53)   2 March 1944

Fol EW, atchd unasgd, WAC Det SU 1740, this sta, are tfrd in gr and asgd to Det C, 3d WAC Tng Cntr, Fort Oglethorpe, Georgia, and will rpt thereat not later than daylight hours, 19 Mar 44, for two (2) weeks of extended field service tng prior to atchmt to Shipment No. RN_200_(C).

Pfc Helen E. Kogel, A704886, (055), WP o/a 5 Mar 44, and is auth 12 day delay

Pvt Allie G. Caison, A200814, (247), WP o/a 10 Mar 44, and is auth 7 day delay enroute, plus 2 days trav time.

Clothing (winter only) and individual equipment as prescribed in TE #21, 10 Mar 43, and chgs thereto, will be taken except that the fol items are auth as indicated:

- Blankets, wool, OD (2 only per individual)

- Canteens will be stainless steel, plastic or aluminum

Fol mailing address will be used:

- Grade, First Name, Middle Initial, Last Name, ASN

- Third WAC Training Center

- Fort Oglethorpe, Georgia

In accordance with AR 35-4520, the FD will pay in advance the prescribed mon alws in lieu of rat a/4 $1.00 per meal for six (6) meals to one (1) person (Kogel).

TO, this sta, will furn nec T for Kogel.

PAC in AR 35-4540, C1, 23 May 42, the FD at destination will pay Pvt Caison mon alws in lieu of trav for the distance fr Ft Crook to destination by the shortest, usually-traveled route a/r 3 cents per mile, regardless of mode of trav, and trav rat for six (6) meals a/r $1.00 per meal and fur rat a/r 67 cents per day.

EW are warned against engaging in conversation, other than official, relative to their origin, destination, or orgn.

TDN. 1-5070 P 431-02 A 0425-24. (Auth: Ltr 7SC, ASF, Omaha, file SPKPE 220.3 (WAC), dtd 28 Feb 44, Sub: Repls for Shipment No. RN_200_(C).)

By order of Maj WATTS:

R. P. HITCHCOCK,

1st Lt., Ord. Dept., Adjutant

OFFICIAL: RESTRICTED

My five-day pass was interesting. I was the only passenger in my car from Sioux City to Lane, South Dakota. The conductor and I spent time visiting and I told him I had to be on this train on Monday morning for my trip to Atlanta.

Monday morning was cold, with temperatures well below zero. My brother's Model A Ford refused to start. He worked and worked and finally got it going. By the time we drove the three miles to the station, the train had pulled out of Lane to the next town of Woonsocket. I asked my brother to drive to the next town to catch the train. We got there, and again the train had left the station. We continued and got ahead of the train. I told my brother after we passed it to pull up at the next train crossing, leave the lights on, and stop on the track—I had to get on that train. He wouldn't stop on the track but did stop next to the crossing and left his lights on. I stood in the middle of the track and waved my arms and heard the whistle blowing, so I knew they saw me. Sure enough, the train stopped and the conductor was at the door, ready to pull me up into the train. The conductor, the same one I had been with five days earlier, said he was watching for me after they left the station in Lane, and when we missed it in the next town, he knew that was me on the track waving my arms. What an experience!

My trip to Fort Oglethorpe in Atlanta, Georgia was uneventful after that dramatic start. We went through special training where we were told we would be working on top secret material. The training by the FBI regarding the top secret work was very intense. We first had to learn how to type without comprehending the details. It's a lesson on concentration. We would be given a page to type and then try to not remember what was in the page. If we could remember, then we knew we hadn't picked up what they were teaching us. We learned how to read word for word without paying attention to the contents or meaning of the material. We were there four or five weeks and every day was the same. Our group was confined to one barrack, which included work space, our own mess hall, and sleeping quarters. We never left that area until we had completed that phase of our training. Even today it is hard to recall that time, because we were being trained not to remember. I have met several FBI agents who told me that type of training was some of the most intense they have ever seen.

Along with that work was the need for a top secret security clearance. When the FBI went to my parents' home to interview them, I'm sure they realized I was going on an unusual assignment. We were issued new uniforms, both summer and winter, and our group, consisting of about thirty WACs—some secretaries and others telephone operators—boarded a train and traveled to Camp Shanks, in New Jersey, for the usual shots and other processing for overseas travel. A few days later, we traveled by bus to New York harbor and boarded the Queen Mary for our trip to England.

Helen left New York on April 9, 1944. In the following letter to her sister, she describes what she experienced:

Dearest Hazel:

It will be several days before I can mail this letter but at least I can start it.

I'm going clear back to my Oglethorpe days. It seems actually years ago, really, instead of weeks. I thought the day would never come when we'd pack up and board that troop train, but we did. It was fun to line up with all the other girls with our full packs, paraphernalia and all, sling them on our backs and all march down to the train, and off we went. That was some life. We ate in a big boxcar that was converted to a dining mess hall. A car at a time would proceed to mess—we would trip, stumble, and fall, often making three point landings until you arrived. Then you stacked your plates as high as you could and then imitated the Hindus by balancing your food. All the time, the train was traveling at a great rate of speed across country and mountains.

We slept in berths. If you were lucky, you slept alone and maybe still more lucky by sleeping in the lower berth. I had an upper and alone, which I didn't mind. We went to bed at 9:00 and got up at 8:00. We spent one Sunday on the train and we had church. One of the girls sang "*Lord's Prayer*" and "*Ave Maria*".

Someone read scriptures, we all sang a few hymns, we all said the Lord's Prayer, and that was all.

Finally we landed at our new destination, eager to find out where it was and how long we would stay there. This camp was somewhere along the eastern shore line. We had beautiful barracks, three to a room, but no sheets or pillow cases. We had to sleep just between two blankets, Army ones at that. And do they scratch! Each day we hoped we would be alerted and put on the boat.

One evening we were told to fall out and march to a big hall. Several companies of girls were leaving and we were going to see them off. As we entered the hall, in columns of twos, everyone in step, the band on the stage started playing—very military and all. When we were all in, the band played a fanfare, the drums rolled, and in entered Colonel Oveta Hobby—oh how the girls clapped! She gave us a few minutes speech about the trip we were undertaking, the hardships we would endure, but how proud she was of all of us, etc.

Then we marched out. The girls who were leaving were fully packed. They boarded the train while we put on a little parade for them. Their noses were pressed against the window panes, tears running down their cheeks, and waved goodbye to us. Though we knew we'd be going shortly, we had to be split up. Every one of us had a special friend in the group. As the train pulled out, the band played "Tiger Rag" and we trudged back to the barracks to sit a while longer.

Finally we were alerted. Before long we were packed and ready for our own ride. We went by boat to the harbor that we were to sail from. This boat travels up and down the eastern shore line and it was a thrill for us to be on it. It was formerly a yacht but converted for war purposes now. It had a ballroom, sun decks, etc.

At last we boarded our steamer for our long awaited trip. As we came down the gangplank of this small boat a war band was there playing a lively tune. We marched so proudly, though our backs were killing us, down the plank, through the shipping dock, and up the plank of our steamer. The Red Cross was there giving us coffee, donuts, and candy. It was very late in the evening and we sure were hungry. We were assigned our cabins, given final orders, and we plopped into bed.

And that is where I'm writing this letter—on the boat crossing the Atlantic Ocean.

Now a little bit of our life on here. It is one of the Queen boats, a luxury liner, the fastest traveling boat there is. In peace time, our particular cabin would cost $1200.00. There are nine of us in this room, three decks high. I sleep in the middle deck. It is quite hot but not too bad. We have one bathroom which is sufficient. We rise in the morning about 9:30. Because of so many troops, we eat twice a day only. Breakfast starts at 6:00 in the morning, but our particular group doesn't eat until nearly 10:00. So why get up earlier. Supper starts at 3:00 in the afternoon but we don't eat until almost 6:00. We spend the day by going on upper decks for fresh air or boat drill—or maybe later on a movie or show.

Most of the time we are confined to our little cabins. We lounge on our beds because we can't move around much. The lieutenants go in the hall and yell, "Anyone wants to go upper deck for a smoke or fresh air for ten minutes". We go up and then back in our rooms again. Because of so many men and so few of us girls, we have men M.P.s guarding our areas completely. Of course we feel like slaves, but common sense tells us they are right.

We saw the Statue of Liberty and New York as we sailed out of the harbor. It was the prettiest sight in the world. Until we see it again, it still remains in our minds.

Till I continue this letter again…

Here's all my love.

The rest of the time we were confined to our quarters, talking among ourselves and wondering what the future held for us. For the first time, I began to realize what being in the Army was about. War was serious business and we were going to be in the middle of the bombing of London. Our ship zigged and zagged to avoid U-boats. Each day we underwent a boat drill, in case we would get hit by a torpedo. There was always a rumor that they spotted an enemy submarine, but we never knew if it was true or not. Eight days after leaving New York, we landed in Perth, Scotland to begin our adventure…

Helen with Robert Young, Kansas 1943

WACs at Fort Des Moines, Iowa 1943

Helen at Fort Des Moines,
Iowa – 1943

Bette, Millie, Helen – Fort
Des Moines, Iowa – learning
recruiting duties - 1943

Bette Millie + I.

Helen home on leave, with her mother, Mary, and sisters, Florence and Hazel

Skelly Award, earned by Philip Kogel, Helen's father,
shown here with his wife, Mary

Helen Kogel, prior to shipment overseas

Queen Mary ship – en route to London

WAC aboard Queen Mary

H.M.S. "QUEEN ELIZABETH" DISPLACEMENT 31,100 TONS.

Pvt. Helen Kogel-A-7044886
Det. Hg Co. Etousa
APO. 887. % P.M. New York, N.y.

POST CARD

FOR CORRESPONDENCE

FOR ADDRESS

"Let us all strive without failing in faith or in duty."—The Prime Minister.

1 June 44.

Hello mom:
I want you to keep
this card for me!!!
As well as all the
others I've sent. Will
have quite a collection
when I get home.
Love
Helen.

Mrs. Phill Kogel
Woonsocket,
South Dakota.
U.S.A.

Censored by
Helen Kogel
Pvt.

U.S. ARMY POSTAL
JUN
3
1944

ENGLAND

A night train ride, with blackout curtains on all windows, took us from our ship in Perth, Scotland to London. Arriving in London, we were billeted in a hotel on Barclay Square, across from the American Embassy. Two girls were assigned to each nicely furnished room. On our first day, we started our routine of eating in an Army mess hall, but enjoyed the English tradition of afternoon tea and scones in the hotel in the late afternoon.

I was assigned to a small office, with a desk, chair, and a manual Royal typewriter. An armed guard stood outside my office and only admitted officers who could present the proper credentials and identification to him. Officers from the Canadian, British, Australian, and US Armies would come in every morning and give me dictation, with my afternoon being spent transcribing my dictation. Every page I typed had to be stamped TOP SECRET, so I knew I was handling extremely confidential material. The name of the project was OVERLORD. I was making three copies of this material and had to use carbon paper (today's copying machines had not been invented yet). My main concern was not making a mistake, since erasing was very difficult. At times, the British officer would take me to the Admiralty, their headquarters, to pick up special material. All of it concerned the movement of troops and supplies which would be involved in the invasion of France.

At the end of each day, the guard would come into my office and take the ribbon from my typewriter and all the carbon paper I had used that day and burn it in the fireplace. One of the officers would pick up the pages I had finished, and he was responsible for them after that. I had no idea who handled the pages and never saw them again until I saw them in the binder that was later given to General Eisenhower. My duty was to type it to the best of my ability. I was never asked to retype a page, or make changes, so I assume my work was satisfactory. After the ribbons and carbon paper was burned, and the pages taken away—then I could leave to return to my quarters in the hotel.

Never did I discuss with my roommate or any of the other girls what I had been working on—nor did they discuss their jobs. It was understood among all of us that we were dealing with highly sensitive and highly classified material. None of us had a "need to know" what the others in our group were doing. We were well indoctrinated with the motto "Loose Lips Sink Ships!" Never would any of us divulge to anyone what our jobs were—and I never talked about it until just before the fiftieth anniversary of the D-Day landing. All we knew and cared about was that we were helping the war effort.

We were experiencing some of the worst V-2 bombings that London had endured. If you could hear the noise the bombs made, you knew you were okay. But if the motor shut off, we immediately got under our desk and covered our heads. When the bombs hit, the whole building would shake and dust flew everywhere. Because the Germans knew where we were working, our compound was often hit. By this time, we were sleeping three stories underground in a bomb shelter in the Square. Every night about dusk (which was around 10:00 PM with wartime double daylight savings time), we would take our blanket and a pillow and head for the shelter. The first floor underground was for people coming in off the street, the second floor was for British people, and the third floor was for the Americans. There was a single cot with a mattress for each of us; we provided the blanket and pillow. Each morning the all clear would sound and we would go back to the hotel, dress, and go to work.

Day after day I sat in my tiny office, officers bringing me more material to include in the operations order I was typing—later to be announced to the world as Operation Overlord, the code name of the invasion of France, or D-Day. Each day the guard came in and repeated the process of taking my ribbon out of my typewriter, collecting all the carbon paper I had used, and burning it in the fireplace. The paper I had typed was taken by an officer and, I assume, locked in a safe. This project kept me busy from late February through April, 1944.

When I finished the project I had been working on, I was asked if I would like to take the final work to General Eisenhower. I jumped at the opportunity and was thrilled that I would get to meet him. We often saw the generals, but only to salute and move on—this was quite an honor for me. When he asked if I knew what I had typed, I assured him I did and was honored to have been trusted with such an important job. He told me that one copy of the order would be sent to General MacArthur, to use as a guide in developing a similar plan for the invasion of Japan.

He then asked me if I knew that I had a brother in England. I told him, "Yes, but I have no idea where he is." He responded with, "We know where he is, and we want you to go see him this weekend." He then handed me a pass and permission to take the train to Salisbury, England, where my brother, Jerry, was stationed as part of the 3rd Armored Division. This was quite a thrill as I hadn't seen Jerry since he left home in 1940, four years earlier. We had a wonderful weekend together. Jerry was given a jeep so we could visit some of the countryside. Saturday night we attended a USO dance where I got to meet a lot of his buddies. I stayed overnight with an English family before boarding a train late Sunday afternoon for the trip back to London.

Following is a copy of the order giving Helen time off to visit her brother…

HEADQUARTERS
EUROPEAN THEATER OF OPERATIONS
UNITED STATES ARMY
OFFICE OF THE CHIEF SIGNAL OFFICER,
APO 887
RCM DIVISION

6 May 1944

SUBJECT: Personnel Off-Duty

To: Commanding Officer, WAC Detachment B

Private First Class Helen E. Kogel, A-704886, is permitted to have time off this afternoon, 6 May 1944, to check travel status.

It would be appreciated if PFC Kogel could be authorized a pass to travel to Salisbury, Wiltshire, tonight and tomorrow, to visit her brother whom she has not seen for 4 years.

Sunday, being her normal day off, will not affect her duty status.

(Signed)

T. J. PALIK

Major, Signal Corps

With my main project complete and while waiting for the invasion to take place, we took advantage of some time off to see the sights of London, such as Madam Tussauds' wax museum, the Tower of London, Shakespeare's home, the Abbey, and, of course, the USO had canteens and dances at some of the largest gardens (as they were called).

One of my highlights in London was the Saturday I stopped by the USO to see what trips were available. We selected a bus trip to Windsor Castle, the home of King George and his family. When we arrived, the King's flag was flying, indicating he was in residence and that we would only be able to view the outbuildings. We saw the chapel, the carriage house, and one large room that had his paintings in it. As we were walking around the room, the door opened and the King, the Queen, and their two daughters, Elizabeth and Margaret, walked in. We were astounded when they came up to us and asked who we were and where we were from. I was the first one in line and when the King approached me, I didn't know whether to kneel or bow or curtsey, or what the procedure was. So I just extended my hand in greeting. Then he introduced his daughters, Elizabeth and Margaret. He asked if I had met Elizabeth since she had just been assigned as a driver for the American Army. Of course I said, "No, I haven't, but I wish her luck. Maybe I'll see her around." Never in my wildest dreams did I ever expect to see the King of England, and the future Queen of England, in my lifetime.

Another interesting experience came when a friend and I saw an invitation on the USO board to visit 10 Downing Street, the home of

Prime Minister Winston Churchill. We arrived just about 4:00 PM, which is the usual time for tea in England. We were invited into a reception room and tea was being served. As we were drinking tea and looking around the room, Mr. Churchill walked in, picked up his cup of tea, and quickly left the room, never saying a word. I wrote to my mother and told her that my afternoon tea was with the Prime Minister of England. (Later, in 1953, he was knighted and became Sir Winston Churchill).

V-2 bombs continued as a daily problem. The bombardment of London kept going without letup. Having our bomb shelter to sleep in was a welcome relief. We could at least sleep through the night without the constant worry of the bombs hitting us.

Late in the evening of June 5, 1944, we heard a heavy volume of Allied planes flying over the city. We quickly suspected that the invasion was starting and the next morning, June 6, 1944, we were convinced it had.

Helen describes her D-Day experiences in a letter to her sister…

Dearest Hazel:

Again I sit down and run off an epistle. Maybe it is because I have to get it off my mind, and writing seems to help.

I don't suppose I'll ever get a chance to send these letters home, but I'm writing anyway.

We are going through one of the periods that is making history—the invasion. 6 June 44.

For three days, we have heard a continual roar of bombers going over the channel. Saturday, Sunday, Monday it woke us up in the morning and put us to sleep at night. Sometimes the noise was so loud it vibrated our windows. We were thankful they were ours and not the Jerries.

So on Tuesday morning, of all days, I pulled K.P. I was awakened at 5:00 by the CQ to go on duty. The planes had started then.

As I walked down the street I had some very good views of the formations. I remember thinking, what a peaceful morning. No one else was up. As I went through Barclay Square, the birds were chirping merrily.

The girls came to breakfast as usual, nothing particular on their minds. We had a small radio turned on in the kitchen, and at 9:15 the announcer asked everyone to stand by—an important announcement was coming. Our officer called all the girls in and we sat around the little radio, not knowing what to expect.

At 9:30, the SHAEF announcer gave Eisenhower's message, "The invasion started at 5:00 this morning." At the very time I was thinking how peaceful it was, boys were setting their feet on the soil of France.

For two hours we sat there listening to the radio. Every country talked to their people in their own tongue. We didn't get hysterical or make any particular noise—it just left a sunken feeling in the pit of our stomachs. I didn't know if Jerry was in there or not.

So the day went on—just another day to many, but to us over here who work in HQ, it meant a lot, not only because we knew people who were in it, but because it was bringing the day very close to when we would pack up and go over, too.

I wasn't satisfied until I could go to the phone and call Jerry to see if he was still there. I couldn't talk to him but I know the people at the R.C. By calling them and asking about him, I'm able to know what is happening. Jerry was still there but for how long, he didn't know.

I'm making plans to go down the first of the week and see him.

Till next time, then…

Having typed up the procedure to be used, I could imagine the devastation the men would endure. I had two friends from my days in

Sherburn, Minnesota who had joined the 82nd Airborne Division. One had stopped in London and visited me only a few days earlier. Later, I heard that both were killed that morning.

We continued our work in London, listening for V-2 bombs with one ear and never getting the thoughts out of our mind about what was happening across the English Channel as the fighting in Normandy, France continued.

From another letter to her sister, Helen describes the bombing in London…

Still another day—

Dearest Hazel:

Again we are going through a hectic period. This time it is more serious because it is affecting us personally—the bombing of London.

It started Thursday night. We had gone to bed just a few minutes. Most of us in PJ's finishing up the last minute things before the 12 o'clock bed check. When all of a sudden the air raid siren blew.

We had heard them before, so thinking just an enemy plane was flying up the Thames river, would be shot, and that's all there would be.

Before we had even had a chance to go down three flights of stairs, the Hyde Park guns went off. That meant the plane was flying over London. The flak was falling right and left around us, because we are only a few blocks from the park. We have one and a half blocks to run for the shelter. I had grabbed a light coat around my PJs, my helmet, and gas mask. I made it to the shelter and found it was pretty well packed. We had a few beds but people were in them already. So I stood up for a while, expecting any minute for the all clear to come.

Then I sat down on the cold concrete floor, still no all clear, but more guns until they even shook the shelter. I was nearly frozen to death, I was so cold. Finally 7:30 in the morning came. Although the all clear hadn't sounded, we were told to hurry and dress and go to work. Not a single wink of sleep, but our jobs had to be performed.

After a hot cup of coffee, we went to the office. How I ever lived the day, was beyond me.

All day long, planes came over and guns roared. They were the pilot-less planes, run by an engine that exploded as it reached the target. They were one ball of fire and usually destroyed the building when they hit. We saw one coming down last night.

The next night we didn't expect to get much sleep again so we went to bed the minute we got off work at 5:30. At 9:30 we were told to go to the shelter again. In the day time you can see what is happening, but at night our only safety is in the shelter. This time I took a couple of blankets to keep warm. We spent the entire night again in the shelter.

And so it keeps up for the third day and night, we have been bombed continually. Maybe an hour between each alert. This morning a bomb fell near here, wrecking blocks of buildings, shaking and breaking windows all over. During church this morning I thought the whole building was going to fall. It surprised me how many people take it so calmly and I was practically under the seat I was so scared.

How much longer is this going to last? I'm beginning to get a little sleep in the shelter, but it isn't sufficient when you have to work hard all day long, too.

I've been to visit Jerry, knowing all the time he would be leaving a matter of a few hours after I left. Already trucks of men and equipment were pulling out. We pretended we didn't notice and went on our way until it was time for me to catch my train home. Then he said he was leaving to write home and tell them because his letters were being held up. But I'm not worrying about him. He's going to be okay.

So that's all for this time...

Toward the end of July, our hotel was hit with a bomb and it was decided we would be safer in France. The morning we were notified that we would be leaving for France, I went across the street to the Telegraph office to send a telegram to my folks to hold up my mail, we would be moving again. While I was writing my telegram, a V2 bomb hit the building. When I woke up, I was laying on the floor, covered with glass and very upset. The officers in the building picked me up and after looking me over told me I wasn't hurt and I could quit crying. I did, but I was still scared and shaken. (In fact, that sensation of the bomb exploding so close stayed with me even after I returned home. If someone slammed a door, I would go into the shakes. It happened a few days after I was home. I was so upset my parents took me to the hospital, about 25 miles away, the closest one to Woonsocket. The doctor put me to sleep with a sedative after my parents told him what happened, and after a good night's sleep, I was much better. They were very careful about making a sudden noise after that). Back to the V2 bomb—I was ready to leave London, and we did that night, July 27, 1944.

The following undated order was given to Helen and the WACs, explaining what they were to take with them...

NOTICE

MONEY Lt Clarke will exchange your English money for French money. You may take with you only 20 shillings in English money. The amount of French money you take is up to your own judgment. Personnel checks are OK to take also American Express checks are OK.

PACKING We are spot inspecting all those who are leaving two days prior to the day you are supposed to leave. Your actual day of departure may and in some instances has been pushed ahead. We will spot inspect nevertheless two days previous to the original date of departure. The actual final packing will be up to you and should be determined when you get definite word from your section when you will leave. Keep out one (1) class A uniform to wear until the last moment.

Pack in your DUFFLE BAG necessary items such as one (1) class A uniform, your blankets, your shelter half, your arctics. Put in your BARRCKS BAG excess items. Pack in your MUSETTE BAG enough personal things to last you for a few days in case you are separated from your baggage, such as toilet articles, wool shirts, etc.

HELMET AND LINER Mark your steel helmet and liner with the prescribed marking—a white strip across the back parallel with the bottom of the helmet. Paint, brush, and stencil may be obtained in the orderly room. Do this immediately (NCO only)

RATIONS Two (2) weeks PX rations may be obtained from WAC PX at any time.

(Signed)

MARGARET A. CLARKE

1st Lt., WAC

Company Commander

Our group of WACs was bused to Southampton and, after dark, boarded a troop ship and crossed the English Channel, destination Utah Beach....

Helen and Jerry Kogel – Late April 1944 – Salisbury, England – On pass given to Helen by General Eisenhower

Three WACs, Helen is on the left

UTAH BEACH

After an uneventful trip across the English Channel, we arrived off the shore around midnight. Told to shoulder our packs, we were then told to disembark by climbing onto a rope ladder, down the side of the ship, to a landing craft that bounced in the water below us. Having never dreamed we would be doing that, it was with quite a bit of trepidation that we climbed over the side, holding on for dear life to the rope ladder, and welcoming the sailor who grabbed our leg to guide us down the final short jump into the landing craft.

Once we were all safely in the landing craft, it pulled away from the mother ship and headed toward the beach, just as it had done many times since the original landings on June 6. I bet the sailors on this small landing craft could have told us a lot of stories from previous landings they had made. We were pleased that our landing was not under hostile fire, the beaches were secure by the time we got there on July 28, 1944. Just like the men before us, we had to wade ashore through waist deep water and wait until morning so we could be picked up and carried to our holding area. Inland from the beach, an enclosed holding area was awaiting us. Small tents had two cots, without mattresses, and a special tent was marked as a female bathing facility.

We were starved, so we happily grabbed our mess kits and headed for the mess tent as daylight started to light the area. Just like the GIs with us, we lined up with our mess kits ready to hold whatever they were serving for breakfast, quite a change from our more civilized eating facilities back in London. I mentioned to my friend in front of me how happy I would be to get out of our wet clothes. A soldier behind us asked where our clothes were. We told him we hoped they were piled up back on the beach by now. We were promised before we left the ship that our duffel bags would be offloaded, brought all the way to the shore so they wouldn't get wet, and be available for us to pick up by daylight. He said he would get his jeep and take us back there to find them.

Little did I know at the time, but that soldier, Staff Sergeant Noel Denton, later was to become my husband.

The front lines were several miles ahead of us. Troops and supplies continued to pour in around the clock. A constant flow of soldiers and supplies moved in from the Channel and up toward the front lines each day. St. Lo had just been taken and the final breakout from the hedgerows in Normandy was not too far away. Fighting still continued and movement was slow as the remnants of the German forces tried to slow the Allied thrust. We lived in tents and ate our meals with the troops.

Utah Beach was my first experience living this close to the front line, and also seeing the devastation left after a battle. It was different from the V-2 and aerial bombings in London. There we saw buildings destroyed and had air raid warnings to take cover. Here we were in the countryside and never knew what type of devastation we would see—dead cattle, homes damaged, church steeples blown down by tanks or artillery firing at a sniper, trees strewn around the area, temporary cemeteries for burying our fallen soldiers, etc.

This is the area where the 4th Infantry Division and the 90th Infantry Division had landed on D-Day, and where the 101st Airborne Division and 82nd Airborne Division had made their parachute landings the night before D-Day. By the time we got there, thousands more troops had landed across that same beach and crossed through the small villages and farmland. Had we gotten there just three days sooner, we would have seen the thousands of bombers flying over as they did the saturation bombing of the German defenses around St. Lo, the beginning of the significant Allied breakout in Operation Cobra, later called the St. Lo Breakout. Sadly, we later found out that over 800 American troops had been killed when bombs fell off target into the American lines.

There was one office building on Utah Beach that was called Headquarters. We stopped by for information or direction, but as far as working at a project, there were none assigned. We were waiting for

Paris to be liberated so we could move in there. Our time was free to come and go within our area. It gave me more time with Noel. Most of the time, we stayed close to the beach. The weather was beautiful and we enjoyed watching the soldiers play ball or whatever they were doing to keep active in their time off.

Noel and I were able to visit Ste. Mere Eglise and see what was left of that town. We also found a farm with two older French people (husband and wife), their daughter and her small children. They had moved their cow into their house during the battle when it surrounded them, but their field had been destroyed and they were having a difficult time finding food. Several times Noel and I drove out there and left them food and supplies that the mess hall had given us. We also found parachutes left behind by the airborne troopers.

My relationship with Noel was very platonic because it was not time to get serious. Neither of us knew what was ahead, and I did not want to experience heartache at a time like this. Not knowing what the future held, we just enjoyed the time we had and hoped for the best. I kept remembering the promise I made my dad to come home for my wedding—he planned to walk me down the aisle. We talked about the future, but Noel was concerned about his future when and if he returned, and whether he would still have a job with a future.

We had freedom to walk around on the beach as long as we didn't venture away from our assigned area limits. This gave me time to get to know Noel. He was a staff sergeant in the Signal Corps and had a group of men under his command. Their job was to support General Eisenhower's headquarters and to ensure communications were established in French villages as the front lines moved closer and closer to Paris.

Other than time spent with Noel, a highlight was the afternoon when Bing Crosby, Bob Hope, and a singer (whose name I don't recall) came to perform for us on the beach.

Despite what started as a platonic relationship, it was during this time when I fell in love with Noel, my future husband. He and his men would go into towns after they had been taken by the Allied forces and set up telephone wires, then come back to the base camp at night. They also were waiting to go to Paris to set up lines in General Eisenhower's office so they could talk to London and Washington.

Dating on a Normandy beach soon after the invasion was not easy, but we figured out a way. We would walk out to a little farm that had apple juice and Cognac. We'd sit on a log and drink and talk.

On 14 August 1944, the following order was given to all WACs on Utah Beach. I wonder if Helen and Noel had any part in causing this to be written...

DETACHMENT A, WAC DETACHMENT HEADQUARTERS COMMUNICATIONS ZONE (FORWARD) APO 886

14 August 44

INSTRUCTIONS TO NEW MEMBERS

WELCOME TO FRANCE! In the time that the WACs have been here they have made an enviable record both in efficiency on the job, and the ease with which they have accepted and adapted themselves to local conditions.

The following points are taken from various Memorandums, Daily Bulletins and the experience of other WACs and will help you to follow the regulations of the camp and avoid difficulties. Read them carefully—know what is expected of you—and continue the high standards of the WACs in Normandy.

1. <u>UNIFORM</u> For duty hours:

• Trousers (outer)

• Jacket, field (optional). If worn, all buttons except first will be buttoned.

- Shirt, wool OD (first button open—sleeves may not be rolled)

- Leggings (at all times outside of WAC area)

- Field shoes and wool socks

- Helmet liner (worn at all times outside of WAC area—straight on head—never carried in hands or under arm)

In off duty hours, uniform is same, except trousers, inner liner, may be worn.

When leaving camp, steel helmet will be worn.

Fatigues may be worn when doing fatigue work, or on day off around WAC area and going to and from Mess.

2. <u>REVILLE</u>

- First call—0600 hours

- Five minute warning—0610 hours

- Reveille—0615 hours. Members will fall in at attention and at normal interval. Within 3 minutes, 1st Sgt will give command "Fall In," and take reports. Any member joining formation after "Fall In" is given is late, and will be so reported by Squad Leader. Uniform will be field shoes, trousers, jacket (buttoned) and helmet liner. Leggings are optional. All members will stand Reveille except the following:

- Sick in Quarters

- Working late (after 2000 hours)

- Day Off

3. <u>INSPECTION</u> Lt. General Lee requires uniformity of living quarters for inspection. All members will follow the SOP

prescribed by this office for arrangement of tents. Tents will be ready for inspection from 0830 to 1630 hrs daily, except Sunday. Members may sleep on day off, but must have area neat and orderly.

4. POLICING AREA Each member must be responsible for policing her own area and picking up papers around the WAC area. This is especially important due to tendency to throw things on grass, thus detracting from general appearance of camp.

5. MAIL The address to be used is:

WAC Detachment, Detachment A

_____Section, Hq Com Z (Fwd)

APO 887, c/o P.M., N.Y.

Mail will be left in sections for censoring and will be delivered to all personnel in the Sections.

6. CAMP RESTRICTIONS Until such time as passes, leaves, and furloughs are granted, no member may leave the camp except on official business. Members will be informed of off-limits areas in each camp.

7. MESS Members will sterilize mess kits before each meal. They will take only as much food as they can eat and no food will be wasted.

The mess hours will be posted for each camp.

8. BED CHECK Call to Quarters at 2245 hrs, and all members will be in the immediate vicinity of the WAC area. Bed check is at 2300 hrs; at which time, all members will be ready for bed and in bed. Quiet will be maintained in all tents after 2300 hrs.

9. BLACKOUT See Bulletin Board for schedule of blackout. This is a very serious matter and no member will light cigarettes,

have fires, or expose any lights after blackout time. It is a court-martial offense to violate blackout regulations.

10. <u>CAMOUFLAGE</u> Wire paths indicate restricted areas. Members will not go in these areas. White clothes will not be exposed at any time.

11. <u>VEHICLES</u> Members will not ride in vehicles except on official business. Helmets will be worn, and members will not sit on sides of jeeps, radiators or running boards.

12. <u>OFF-LIMITS</u> The living quarters of EM, WAC officers, and Army Officers are off limits at all times to WAC personnel.

13. <u>DAILY BULLETIN</u> A Daily Bulletin from this office is posted every day. All members are responsible for reading this Bulletin, initialing names when they appear on Bulletin Board and reading other notices. Any changes to these instructions will be posted on the Bulletin Board.

KEEP UP THE NAME OF THE WACS IN FRANCE

(Signed)

ISABEL B. KANE
Capt., WAC
Commanding

Two fellow WACs in front of a jeep as they wait near Utah Beach in August 1944 for Paris to be liberated so they can move to Paris.

PARIS

On August 25, 1944, Paris was liberated. Although the French 2nd Armored Division has taken credit for the liberation, those who were there, including General Omar Bradley, know that the 12th Infantry Regiment of the 4th Infantry Division had a key part in the liberation, along with other American troops who followed closely in their footsteps.

General Bradley wrote in his book, *A Soldier's Story*: "To hell with prestige," I finally told Allen, "tell the 4th (Infantry Division) to slam in (to Paris) and take the liberation." Learning of these orders and fearing an affront to France, LeClerc's French 2nd Armored Division mounted their tanks and burned up their treads on the brick roads to enter Paris.

As the French 2nd Armored Division entered Paris and mingled with men of the 4th Infantry Division's 12th Infantry Regiment, it was common to see their tanks abandoned as the French soldiers disappeared into the bars and brothels of Paris. Soldiers of the 12th Infantry Regiment pressed on to take out the remaining German hot spots and snipers.

In Colonel Gerden Johnson's book, *History of the 12th Infantry Regiment in WWII*, originally published in 1947, he wrote: ...The significant date flashed through the minds of the men and brought home with startling impact how much battle had been crowded into two short months of the 12th Infantry's drive—June 6, D-Day; June 25, Cherbourg; July 25, the (St. Lo) breakthrough; and now August 25—Paris!

At 1230, Colonel James S. Luckett, commander of the 12th Infantry Regiment, contacted Colonel Billotte of General LeClerc's French Army Staff, and the Police Prefect Captain Edgard Pisani, at the Prefecture of Police located opposite Notre Dame Cathedral. The colonel was informed of a show of resistance in a German barracks near Palais de la Republique. Colonel Luckett, Major Lindner, and four enlisted men armed with tommy guns hopped into their jeeps and proceeded with some difficulty to the area in question. At the Palais de la Republique,

French Second Armored forces were firing at the bullet spattered barracks nearby. A short truce was arranged. Terms were discussed with the besieged German commander, General von Chaulitz. The Nazi would not surrender without a show of arms—a matter of honor. Thereupon both parties retired to their cover and fired their weapons. At 1300, the German general surrendered and was taken into custody by the French. He was returned under heavy guard to the Prefecture of Police. Colonel Luckett then returned to the Montparnasse railroad station where General LeClerc and the American V Corps commander, General Leonard T. Gerow, were located. He was told by General Gerow just what sectors of Paris to clear.

It was evident that had it not been for the timely arrival of the men and the supporting weapons of the 12th Regimental Combat Team, the small isolated pockets of German resistance would have developed into a strong threat to vital bridges and communication links in the city. However, Paris, the capital city, belongs to the French. Hence the capitulation of Nazi officials to General LeClerc in Montparnasse at 1700 hours...

Soon after Paris was liberated, Helen and her fellow WACs entered Paris, as shown in this article from a South Dakota newspaper:

Jerauld County WAC Among First in Paris

Paris, France—(Delayed)—Laden with full packs, bed roll, and gas masks, the first WACs arrived here by truck just a week after the capital had been liberated. French men and women lined the sidewalks, cheering, waving and shaking hands with the WACs at every opportunity.

Gazing wistfully at the gay clothes of the French women, one travel-weary WAC remarked, "I'd always dreamed of going to Paris someday, but I never thought that I'd look like this when I arrived."

The WACs will serve as telephone operators, jeep drivers, statisticians, draftsmen, secretaries, and interpreters.

Among the first WACs to arrive were three South Dakotans. They were Pvt. Ruby Nicholl and S/Sgt. Ruth Herdman, both of Custer, and Pfc. Helen Kogel, of Wessington Springs.

Helen continues with her story...

Soon after Paris was liberated, we were flown into Paris on a cargo plane, landing at the main airport. We traveled by bus to our hotel in Paris. There was still sporadic fighting in the streets so we were confined to our quarters for three days. There was no food available for us so we all pooled our K-rations and made do until the truck arrived from the mess hall. Noel happened to drive the supply truck that brought us our food. His unit was assigned to Paris to ensure the central telephone office was not booby trapped by the Germans on their way out. Paris streets were still filled with Parisians of all ages celebrating their freedom.

The room I was assigned to had a surprise in it: a German officer's clothes were still in the closet. It didn't take long for me to call the hotel manager to come and clear out those uniforms. I didn't want him to come back and find me there.

As soon as we were settled, we were able to open up our office and meet the group we would be working for. We set about getting General Eisenhower's headquarters set up and went back to work.

Our first hotel was very rundown. We stayed there a month and then moved to another upscale hotel, just off the Champs Elysees. That was a very good place to stay, an excellent hotel where we stayed until the end of the war.

Working in Paris was different. All of us girls were put into one room, an office pool, where an officer could request any of us to work for him. I wouldn't say it was Top Secret work, but I do remember one of the officers was tracking a submarine, and we were fascinated to watch how he was able to have a warship sink it.

We were allowed to use our spare time, especially on the weekends, to visit all the great museums and places of interest. Seeing places I had read about in my history books at school made me realize what a wonderful opportunity I had been given. Seeing the Louvre, the Eiffel Tower, the Arc de Triomphe, Notre Dame, the Versailles Palace, the whole city was something to see.

Noel was with the Signal Corps and stayed in Paris for about four weeks, making sure all communications were set up and working properly. We had time to meet after work and get better acquainted. His outfit would follow a unit that would clear a town, and then they would make sure there was telephone service back to the headquarters in Paris. Even after he went on to the front lines, he would call me late at night, usually at midnight, when the lines were clear of other traffic. We both knew girls in the central telephone office that would pass his calls through. It was our way of keeping in touch. He would tell me where he was and what happened each day, so I could write his mother for him. His letters were always censored and I could keep her informed without letting his exact location be known.

Noel was good looking and a great cook. He was also a nice gentleman. I was attracted to his manners and the way he cared for his mother. A man who respects his mother respects his wife.

Noel and I had a great dating experience. We went to dances on the weekends and to the movies. There was a lot of entertainment to choose from once Paris became the hub of the Allied headquarters. The only things lacking in the city were the restaurants. Paris didn't have any food at that time. The USO provided food though, and we were grateful. We did have a favorite meeting place, at one of Paris' famous outdoor corner cafes.

Liberated Paris was a wonderful experience. It was the main place for the military to send troops for rest and relaxation (R&R). The USO provided very large living and eating quarters for all of them to use. There were plenty of activities, including the latest movies and a canteen for dancing, especially on the weekends. Tickets to all the special shows were available. We took in the Follies and other dancing programs. I missed a great opportunity—shopping in the large department stores. It was because I didn't need anything. The Army forced us to wear our uniform at all times, and I was not good in their money exchange and did not understand the French language, so I stayed away from the department stores. I did use the hair salons and perfume shops of Paris, so I didn't miss out on everything.

I did buy a hat and sent it to my mother on her birthday. After I returned home, I asked her how she liked the hat. I thought she would wear it to some of her meetings, but she said it was so unusual, compared to what they wore during the rationing days of the war, that she gave it to my sister to redesign into something not as flamboyant.

I had very little contact with troops coming into Paris, other than meeting them at USO dances. I did associate with those that I worked with. We often used the bicycles available at our hotel to visit parks and interesting places not available by the Metro. Their transportation was great to most places. Several of us visited Versailles, where the armistice ending WWI was signed. We also took a boat trip down the Seine River.

I loved to dance at the USO. The jitter bug was the dance we all enjoyed. I wore a pair of shoes out and had to have them replaced.

One of the highlights in Paris was when we were informed that the hotel where the officers were billeted had invited the Glenn Miller Orchestra to play, and we girls were invited to join them. Tex Benike brought the band over from London and was directing them. We kept asking when Glenn Miller was going to arrive. We didn't learn until the next morning that his plane disappeared over the Channel and was never recovered.

Other than the Glenn Miller band, I didn't meet any famous people, not even General Eisenhower other than seeing him at a distance as he entered the headquarters. I did not know or hear about Kaye Summersby, his driver, until she wrote her book. I did read in another book that the General's adjutant wrote saying she was part of his office, but she was more involved with an officer on the front lines. I can't speculate about the often-quoted story linking General Eisenhower and his driver together romantically. I've also been asked if I had my picture taken with General Eisenhower. Of course I didn't—corporals don't go up to generals asking to have their picture taken with them.

I met a Parisian girl, Nicole, who became a good friend. She was having a hard time and I would meet her and give her my chocolate candy and cigarettes to barter for food. One day she invited me to her apartment (one room with kitchenette and bath) for lunch. She had picked some mushrooms from an underground field. We had steamed mushrooms, French bread, and a glass of wine. That's the way a lot of the people survived.

I'll always remember the Battle of the Bulge and how intense our office was for several weeks. With the German troops impersonating Americans, our headquarters initiated very tight security where our ID was checked and a challenge and password was used every time we came into our building—even for those of us the guards saw every day. It wasn't until we heard that the first group of Americans had reached the besieged troops and could deliver supplies and reinforcements to them that things started to relax a bit. With the need for more infantry soldiers, many of the men working in and around Paris in support roles were retrained and pressed into the infantry after the Bulge was stopped and the Germans began retreating again.

As the war started to wind down and news of liberations of our prisoners of war and the death camps came into the news, Helen wrote the following to her brother, Everett:

May 1, 1945

… We believe something will crack within the next few days. But even if it does, I don't see how they can relieve us and send us home right away. I know Jerry, and even Clem, will get home before I do. But I don't mind—Jerry really deserves that trip before me—and I hope he gets it soon.

Have the papers been playing up this liberation of the Allies? The stories our boys tell when they come back from the front, really makes a person sick. Jerry wrote and said that of all the things he has seen in this war, the one he'll remember the longest was the sight of the boys his outfit liberated. He said even grown men cried when they saw the Americans. Has any word been received on Sam Lillahag? I have been making contacts with the Adjutant General's office who handle the list of US boys liberated. I asked them to watch for his name, but it can easily slip by without them knowing. I imagine he will be in the hospital for some time when he does get freed.

All my love to the best family in the world,

Your sis—Helen

On VE Day, Helen wrote the following letter to her parents:

May 8, 1945

Dearest Mom and Dad:

This is V-E day here in Paris! Words can't describe what is all happening. It is 5 o'clock, and I am here in the office working. All the others took off and left me holding down the fort until 5:30 then I can go home, too.

At 2 o'clock a dozen of us were picked to go to the Trocodero, which is a huge auditorium. We heard President Truman's speech direct from the States at 3 o'clock, several speeches by other generals, we sang, heard a couple of chaplains give a prayer and then we came home, or rather back to the office.

Last night at 11 o'clock the celebrating began. The lights on Notre Dame, Sacre Cuer, The Arc, and part of the street lights went on. About a dozen planes kept flying in the air and dropping flares of all colors to light up the sky. I had been washing clothes when the girls called me to come up to the top of the roof of our hotel and watch the fireworks. I'm telling you it was a sight I will never forget. It was the Fourth of July, Christmas, and New Year's celebrations all put into one. The people just jammed all of Champs Elysees. Until nearly morning we could still hear them yelling. Then this morning the streets were one mass of flags and bright colors. At noon, all the outdoor cafes and bars were packed with people celebrating already. At noon when I went home I was nearly crushed in a mass of kids that were staging a parade of their own. They had just come from school, nearly 2,000 of them. They reached for two and a half blocks long, just packed together. They were singing and marched all around the US Headquarters then on up to the Arc and down Champs Elysees. They stopped all traffic and made everyone stand back until they had passed.

Tonight will be one mad mob. The French have proclaimed today, tomorrow, and Thursday as holidays. And they intend to keep on celebrating until then, which means we won't get much sleep at night, because we live just a half block off Champs Elysees.

I am going to church tonight, and afterwards see the town myself. We have five more weeks of our Novena. This one is lasting thirteen weeks. We started the week before Palm Sunday. That is one reason I'm glad you live in town, now you can go to all those things, too.

It is funny. I never would have thought that I would make Novenas, Missions, Communion the first Friday and Sunday of every month like this, on my own. Remember how you used to have to nearly knock us down to go to church when we were kids. Now, my Sunday is spoiled if I don't go to church. We can go every half hour until noon, and then if we miss we can go at 4:30 or 6 o'clock and still hear high mass. They really do everything they can to accommodate the soldiers here in Paris. But I guess that is because 90% of the French are Catholics and there is a church on every corner. But I enjoy church, and I know I'll be a darn good member when I get back to civilian life again.

I don't know what will be happening to me after this. I know our Headquarters will be breaking up soon. A lot of our boys are combat men who have been here three years or more, served their time in combat, were injured and were put in limited service over here. They will all be going home, of course. All the French civilian help will be released, all the British civilian girls we brought over here from England with us will be going home, and that will leave just a very few of us. It will be a draw between working in another outfit here in Paris or moving on to Germany. Of course, if I can't come home, I'd much rather stay here in Paris where we have nice accommodations, because in Germany, that means living in tents, mud, and eating out of canteens. There aren't any cities large enough for a headquarters to be set up. We'd have to pick some big pasture and use temporary buildings and tents for offices. Which isn't so nice.

Jerry, of course, will be coming home very soon. He has been in combat since June 12th, which is nearly 11 months. I don't know whether he will be discharged or be trained for the Pacific. Because he has never been wounded, he will have a hard time getting a discharge, which seems awful funny, doesn't it.

I received a letter from him yesterday saying that he expected a furlough to Paris soon, which will suit both of us.

My furlough is coming up next month. I am making plans to go to the Riviera, if the girls I run around with can get off then, too. We only have two places to go. England or the Riviera. Boy, oh, boy, can I ever use a week of rest. My nerves are getting so bad, they nearly run me out of the office, or rather I nearly run them out. I have been snapping everyone's head off for no reason at all. It is just that you can't relax at all, no matter how hard you try. Even at night.

I was hoping I could send some money home this month, but it doesn't look like I can. I want to save a little for my furlough, but maybe at the end of the month I can send $50 or so home. How much is my bank account now? You have never said whether that $100 money order reached you or not. Be sure and tell me in your next letter. I don't want that to get lost.

I must close now, and get my work put away.

All my love for now:

Your daughter

P.S. I'm glad to be able to have a part in VE-day over here where it means so much more. But the real V-day, I'd love to be home with you and Dad. Maybe!

I witnessed the lights coming back on in Paris from the rooftop of my hotel with other WAC friends, as well as the Victory Day celebration. The day after the lights were turned on, we marched in a parade down the Champs Elysees. We were told to polish our shoes and our buttons and press our uniforms because we would be marching down the Champs Elysees with all the other military units representing every country that was involved in the war. It was thrilling. It lasted at least five or six hours and included equipment that was used by everyone. Our girls marched until we passed the reviewing stand and then we dropped out so we could see the rest of the parade.

And five days later, she wrote this more detailed letter to her sister, which was returned to Helen by the censors—she kept it so we can now include all the details she wrote back then:

12 May 1945

... Well Hazel, the War is over. Period. I wish I could tell you the news you are waiting to hear, but I can't. Yesterday when the point system was announced, we frantically counted up ours, and sure enough, I had just 44. I wanted to have the day off to go home and pack my bag. Then today the *Stars and Stripes* comes out with a nice slap in the face, saying the WACs have been considered essential and will be put in the Army of Occupation in Germany until six months after the defeat of Germany or until they can be released. Course that will mean one to three more years over here. Well, our sails surely were deflated. The Army really does some queer things, and this is another of them. Of course that was today, maybe tomorrow they will say something else. One girl who works at the headquarters still swears that we old timers are going home very soon. The paper can be wrong.

Yes, the war is really over, but if you had been here in Paris for the celebration, you would have thought that life was just beginning. I have never been to such a mad, exciting, completely out of the world jamboree. It was the Fourth of July, Christmas, New Year's and all the State Fairs put together. It started Monday night about 10 o'clock when the first news came over the radio. Whistles blew, churches rang their bells, and the sky was filled with planes shooting every color of flares they could. All the lights went on over the city. The crowd just screamed for hours. I had gone home right after work and washed and put up my hair. I had my radio on and heard the first news at 7 o'clock. I called Joe at the office and he said it wasn't true. Then at 10 o'clock I heard it again and rushed up to the girls who room on the top floor. We went up on the roof and were able to get the first glimpse of the city as the lights went on. It is a thrill I shall never forget. After being over here a year or more and going through city after city that was pitch dark, then to see a large city like Paris turn on their lights, section by section, it was unbelievable. Just like a big Christmas tree. We had a wonderful view of the sky and of the flares.

Tuesday the city started early and kept it up all day and night. At noon, I was nearly choked or trampled to death. One of the schools was dismissed for the week and the kids staged a parade, surrounding our offices and singing and yelling, at least 2,000 kids. They extended for nearly four blocks, just a solid mass of them. At 5:30 when we went home, it was in full swing. People kissing everyone on the cheeks, especially the French kissing the American soldiers. Wonderful—I even got a few. I was on my way to church that night, my regular Novena at the church, when about 6 GIs spotted me and cornered me, and before they finished, French men and women pitched in and formed a circle around me and sang and wanted me to join their conga line that would go all over Paris, but I was nearly late for church and I couldn't get loose, until a couple of MPs saw my plight and rescued me by putting me on their shoulders and carrying me away. Anyway, I made it to church on time. But you can't get angry, not when everyone was so happy and in such a celebrating mood.

Wednesday was the same, and even Thursday. Thursday night was the last evening and Friday morning stores and businesses opened up again, only the city sure looked like it had been dragged through a knot hole. Did I celebrate? Not like everyone else. We didn't have bed check Tuesday or Wednesday night, so Tuesday night, Joe took me to the Officers Club dance, we had three glasses of champagne the whole evening. It wasn't even 12 when I got to bed, and Wednesday night I was in bed by 11:30. Seems funny, after going to bed before 12 for 2 ½ years, you get too tired to stay out later. Then too, we had to work the next day, so there wasn't much sense in getting tight and staying up all night.

But that is all over now, people are back to normal as well as their heads, and we still go to work every day just as though nothing has ever happened. We'll be doing the same for the next year, I guess.

(The censor XX'd this paragraph out—but it is still readable) Notice the picture on the top of this letter. I picked this sheet for you so you could see what the fountains look like. All over the city of Paris, they have fountains springing water, on every other street or so. They had been turned off for five years until VE day, and then they were fixed up and turned on, boy, they really are pretty, at night they have bulbs inside of the fountain so that it is all lit up. Very beautiful.

Monday is the third anniversary of the WACs. Paris is really opening their doors to us and giving us a celebration. There are over 2,000 of us here in Paris and outskirts. We are staging a parade at 11 o'clock down Champs Elysees. The first parade the American Army has given in France, other than the passing of the troops through Paris on Liberation Day. Generals of all kinds will be here to review us. You will probably see pictures of it in the papers and in the newsreels. *(censors XXd the following sentences out, too)* We have been practicing every other night for the past two weeks for this thing, and it should be good. We are wearing our uniforms and yellow gloves and scarfs.

(The censor XX'd this paragraph out—and most of the following two paragraphs) I had a rather nice surprise last night. We were drilling for the parade when I noticed a WAC officer who looked awful familiar. Sure enough, it was one of my recruiting officers. She sure was glad to see me and wants me to be sure to come over to her headquarters to see her. She just arrived a month ago from the States and is stationed here in Paris.

I received a letter from Jerry yesterday. He is fine, and had lots of news. He said an old CO of his back in England who had been injured while crossing France and had been hospitalized in England had just joined their company again and was the CO. I had met him several times while visiting Jerry in England. Jerry and Swanny had a party for Lt. Parks when they found out he had just arrived. Swanny baked four pies, baking powder biscuits, creamed tuna fish, and French fries, besides liquor. Parks asked about me, and then he told Jerry he'd do all he could to get him either a pass or furlough to see me. So Jerry said just hold tight and maybe he'd be seeing me.

Jerry hasn't enough points to get a discharge but I have a very good idea that you will be seeing him soon. So get your good clothes on and really throw a big party for him, he deserves it. At least he'll get a 30 day furlough before he starts on further training.

I guess I have rattled on enough, had better stop and finish up my work. Please write soon and tell me all about Guy. I wish you could take more pictures, I bet he has grown a lot since the last ones. I was hoping I could get home in time to help with fall harvesting, you could use an extra hand, I'll bet. Oh well, we'll see, maybe I'll buzz in and surprise you all. If I do come home it will be with a discharge that is for sure. They can't make me stay in any longer once I get back to the States.

By for now, all my love, and a happy birthday,

Your sis, Helen

With the war in Europe over, Helen was feeling both feisty and melancholy as she wrote the following letter to her parents:

June 4, 1945

Dearest Mom & Dad:

Hello you two lucky people—How badly do you want to see your son and daughter? Jerry and I talked to "Ike" the other day and after discussing the situation over thoroughly we decided to make it home for Dad's birthday—so you'd better kill the fatted calf. We sure are dying for some good "Kogel Steaks".

Don't get your hopes up too high, though, but it is beginning to look very favorable for me. They are giving us a choice of CBI (China, Burma, India), Germany, or home with a discharge. I don't need to tell you what my choice is. All I want to do is to see your smiling faces again.

Jerry is coming into Paris soon on a furlough. I only hope he makes it before we move to Germany. I think we'll be leaving the 15th of this month. That doesn't mean I'll stay there. They are sending the girls with the highest points home first, so as my number comes up, I'll leave. Transportation facilities are the biggest drawback…

Mom, I was thinking tonight. How very lucky we Kogels are. Our prayers have been answered, haven't they? To think of what Jerry has been through and come out without a scratch. My experiences haven't been anything, and now we are coming home. Just stop and think how other people will feel when all the boys come home and that place is empty in their home. Clem still has quite a bit of time to put in, but his chances are much better than the earlier boys. It isn't very likely anything will hurt him. You've never regretted having a big family, have you? I know you have had your share of worry—it's only natural if you love us, but believe me, there hasn't been a time that we haven't been proud of our folks.

Oh Mom—Honestly, I can hardly wait until I get home.

I guess I'd better close. Keep writing and here's hoping…

Your loving daughter

Helen

Another wonderful opportunity I had was an auto trip that four of us took, touring Europe. This included my roommate and two other soldiers we were working with. Since I had a driver's license from the military, we were given a car and toured part of France, Belgium, and Holland and then back through France and visited Rheimes where the peace treaty was signed and then back to Paris.

With the anticipation of going home, I bought lots of French perfume at a very reasonable price, plus other small items that served as wonderful reminders of the great memories of my time serving in Paris.

Another letter to her parents shows the frustration the GIs felt as the war was over and they were still overseas…

28 July 1945

Dearest Mom:

Do you mind if I have a little chat with you tonight? Seems ages since I've written, though actually it has only been a couple of days. But I guess you don't mind the letters coming often, do you?

I can't understand why everyone has stopped writing to us over here. Just because the war is over doesn't mean we are on our way home. I'll have many more months over here. I know that I'm terribly sorry I built your hopes so high at first. It is all my fault. I thought things would be different but the WACs will be the last to leave Europe. The boys are needed at home and in the Pacific so naturally they get first priority. But, Darling Mother, no matter how long I stay, it just makes home that much more important, and some day when I do come, I'll make up for all the time I've been gone. We can have our talks and work together, go places, and you'll forget I've ever been away...

I have finally come to the conclusion that the Lord is certainly watching over me (though he must be having a trying time). Last Saturday night I was invited to Nicole's place (this French girl friend of mine). She had several guests besides me. After a nice dinner she wanted to show me her new motorcycle. Over here it is impossible to buy a car so she got a motorcycle. We made lots of plans about going all over the country now that she has it. So she asked if I'd get on the back (it had an extra seat in the back) and we'd try it out. So on I jumped. We went around the block once and she was kinda wobbly trying to balance us both so we went around again. As we turned the corner she thought she put the brakes on but it was the gas and as we whirled around, I toppled off, landing on my head, knocking myself out. Luckily, there was a French hospital near and they came out and took me in. Nothing was broken but I am again nursing a bruised back and skinned up legs. You'd think I'd grow up, wouldn't you? Poor Nicole had hysterics, she thought she had killed me. That's the first I heard—her sobbing. So I wasn't slow about showing them I could walk and got out of there in a hurry...

7 Aug '45

My Dearest Mother:

Am leaving at midnight tonight on my furlough. Another girl, Janie Stayfield, is going with me. She is a very nice girl, quite small, quiet, and just my type. She rooms just next to me.

We get on the train at 12 midnight and go to Dieppe, arriving about 5:00 in the morning then get on that boat that takes us across the Channel to Southampton about 10 o'clock. From there another train to London; arriving about noon. We'll spend maybe a day and then go on up to Glasgow, Scotland and spend about three or four days traveling all over Scotland, and possibly Ireland if we can swing an airplane ride.

Of course I'll be writing every day or so while I'm gone so you'll know what I am doing. Oh Mother, how I wish you were here to go with me. Maybe we can travel once in a while when I get home. I'm a veteran at it now and we would have so much fun. Anyway, as long as you aren't able to be with me, I'll describe everything in detail so you will know what it is like. Scotland is really a beautiful country and the people just can't do enough for you. That was the way when we first landed in Scotland a year and a half ago. Heavens, it seems like ages ago.

So, Dear One, till the next time…

Goodnight,

Your daughter, Helen

From a letter Helen mailed to her parents…

26 Aug '45

Dearest Mom & Dad:

Here is the letter I've been waiting to write. I have dreamed of coming home for a long time and now it is coming true.

I still can't tell you the exact date we'll be leaving but one group leaves between 10-15 Sept and the other group around the 25th. We are supposed to fly if weather permits. I'm keeping my fingers crossed hoping I'll be on the first shipment. All my friends left yesterday. Remember the girl who went on furlough with me? She went home, too.

Several months ago I mentioned the fact that I'd like to go out to the farm first when I come home. That isn't hurting your feelings, is it, Mom? I do like the idea of living in town, but I know the whole family will be together the first night and I'd like it to be in the house I remember, then I can look around and see the same house, same people that I have dreamed so much about.

I insist you and Dad meeting me. You were the ones who saw me off the last time. I may fly from Minneapolis to Huron if I can. If not, I'll take the train to Woonsocket, and you can meet me there.

I'm writing this in bed, it is Sunday morning and I don't have to go to work, so I'm taking it easy. In a little while I'll get up, press my suit, and go to church. This afternoon several of us girls are going dancing and probably again in the evening. I sure go dancing a lot.

Do you think Cecil and Marion and kids can come up home when Jerry and I get there or will we have to go to Minnesota to see them? I don't know how they are giving out discharges. Some say we get a 30 day furlough as soon as we hit New York, then report back to camp to get processed and discharged. Oh well, that will take care of itself. Right now I'm just interested in getting home.

Will keep the letters coming thick and fast for awhile so you will know what is going on. Jerry expects to leave about the 1st of Sept. It will be a race between us two to see who gets home first.

Must close now.

All my love,

Your returning daughter—Helen

2 Sept '45

Paris, France

My Dearest Mom:

Time to send another letter your way. Here it is Sunday. Didn't do very much today. My girl friend, Joie ((Josephine Anspaugh) and I went dancing last night, so this morning we slept until almost 9 o'clock, then made a mad dash for the dining room so we'd get a cup of coffee before it closed. Then we dressed and I went with her to Protestant church at 9:30 and then she went to mass with me at 11 o'clock. Awful religious, aren't we? Church twice in one day. She was down in my room all afternoon sleeping, and tonight we are going dancing again. Tomorrow is Labor Day and a holiday for us. No work, oh boy! Don't know yet what we'll do, probably mend and clean clothes. That is always a job that is never complete. We seem to always have clothes to fix.

Rumors have it that we'll leave sooner than the 25th, but I can't put much faith in them. If we do leave sooner, then my trip to Germany and Holland will be off, and I'm planning quite strongly on going up there. But, guess I'll just have to wait and see.

Mom, I have been wondering what I'll do about clothes when I get home. Maybe I had better spend a couple days in New York and buy a few things. I'll bet I haven't a stitch of clothes left, have I? I do have a blue suit and hat, haven't I? Or is that gone? I won't be able to keep anything except one suit and a few underclothes (khaki) which I don't intend wearing the minute I get home.

I have an idea clothes aren't easy to buy in Huron or Mitchell, so I think I'll do that. I want some high heeled shoes, three or four dresses, purse, underclothes, and etc. What do you think, Mom?

Don't mind too much if I'm an awful clothes hound for the first month or two. But being in London and especially Paris where the clothes creations are out of this world… well, you get such a craving for pretty dresses and fancy hats, having worn the same suit for three years. It will probably drive me crazy. All I can think of is buying the slinkiest dress and the craziest hat you have ever seen. I'm so tired of shirt, tie, and a suit. When I once take my uniform off, I never want to put it on again. I wonder now—whether it was wise to give all my clothes away.

Mother Dear, it won't be long now. Each morning when I wake up, I say, "One more day closer to home." It is just like counting the days until Christmas, only coming home is better.

Last night I dreamed about the house. I could see every room and the way the furniture looks. I am very curious to see if it looks like that or if it will be different. It is exciting to know I'm coming home to a house I have never seen, except from the outside. Just so you and Dad and the boys are there, that's all I care.

So, till next time…

Your daughter,

Helen

P.S. Today is the official VJ Day—wonderful, isn't it?

In September, I was sent to Frankfurt, Germany to record transcripts from prisoner of war interrogations. The only one I can remember was a scientist from the Leica Camera Company. We wanted to know why and how their camera could see at night. That's the first I ever heard about infrared cameras.

American troops of the 4th Infantry Division arriving in Paris, August 25, 1944

Some German equipment destroyed during the liberation of Paris

German Prisoners of War being marched to a POW camp – August 25, 1944

Liberation parade in Paris, Champs-Élysées – August 29, 1944 – Troops are the newly arrived U.S. 28th Infantry Division

Troops of U.S. 28th Infantry Division in Liberation parade in Paris,
Champs-Elysees – August 29,1944

French General Charles DeGaulle and American General Omar Bradley reviewing troops during the Paris liberation parade, August 29, 1944.

ABOVE: Entering Paris - August 1944
RIGHT: Noel

LEFT: General DeGaulle
RIGHT: Helen in Paris

Flower Wagon in Paris

Helen at a flower wagon in Paris

Helen visiting the
Palace of Versailles

With WAC friends, and Soldiers, in
Paris – Helen is in the middle

Patch worn by Helen

A casual walk along the Champs-Élysées in Paris, fall of 1944

Helen riding a bicycle outside Paris, the hotel
had bicycles the WACs could borrow

Helen's brother, Jerry Kogel, in the middle while on an R&R pass to Paris from the front lines, 1945

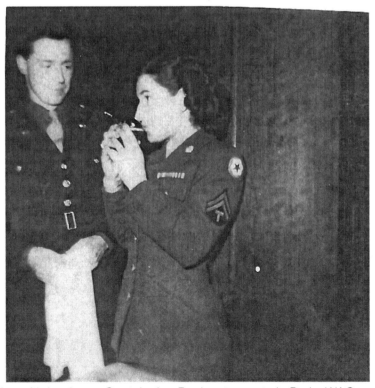

Helen with her boss, Captain Joe Doyle, at a party in Paris. WACs were commonly invited to these parties given by officers.

Eiffel Tower

French women in Paris. Bicycles were a common form of transportation.

Corner café where Helen often met Noel when he was in Paris and not near the front lines.

Noel Denton near the end of WWII

WACs in V-E Day parade in Paris, May 1945 –
Helen is the 7th WAC in the left hand file

WAC officers on the reviewing stand at V-E Day parade, May 1945

V-E Day parade, taken from Helen's hotel window. All Allied nations participated in the day long parade.

FINALLY HOME

In October, we were finally informed that it was time for us to pack up and return home. We took a bus to LeHavre, France and crossed the Channel on a large boat to Southampton and boarded the Queen Elizabeth and crossed to the New York harbor. From there we took the train to Fort Des Moines, Iowa, the same place I had trained in 1943. We were given a chance to call our family and inform them we were back in the States and would be returning home.

The next day I took the train to Woonsocket and my sister, Hazel, met me at the station. All available family members were waiting for me as I arrived at my parents' house in Woonsocket. My brothers and sister didn't return until a month later but we were all together on New Year's Day, 1946.

The first thing I had to do was to get acquainted with the house in Woonsocket, which was a lot different from the farm—especially the indoor plumbing and electricity. My parents took me shopping because my sister was able to wear my clothes and had taken most of them. Silk stockings were still hard to find but we found some. Thank goodness I could get rid of those old cotton stockings we wore in the Army.

I was able to get a job with the local creamery doing their office work. Noel had his job waiting for him with Southern Bell in Jonesboro, Georgia, but he had to wait until his salary increased enough for us to be married. We kept in constant communication through the telephone. In February, 1946, he took a week off and flew up to South Dakota to meet my family and ask me to marry him. He couldn't find an apartment in Georgia and so he was living with his aunt, who also worked for Southern Bell. We made arrangements to have our church wedding on April 22, 1946 when he and his aunt came back up to South Dakota.

My oldest brother and sister were our best man and maid of honor, with two other brothers and my other sister as attendants.

An event happened that stayed with me the rest of my life. The local train played a big part. Before the ceremony, I was waiting for the beautiful flowers to arrive, but the train had come to town and stopped, closing the only street to reach the church. I had no bridal bouquet. My attendants had already walked down the aisle and I was waiting with my father for my flowers. The wedding march had already played once. My father gave me a good shake and told me if this was the only disappointment I would ever experience in my life I had better start walking down the aisle. I did but cried all the way. That message he gave me has stayed with me from then on. In later life, when our house burned, when Noel had several serious illnesses, and, of course, when my entire family died, his words always gave me the strength that you can survive.

My folks had the wedding reception and wedding dinner at our home with all my relatives and friends in attendance. Later that evening, my brother took us to the airport in Huron and we took the first flight to Sioux Falls, then on to Atlanta, and then down to Florida where I met his mother and stepdad for the first time.

Because we couldn't find an apartment, we lived with his aunt until we found a one bedroom apartment, but had a very difficult time getting furniture. Finding a stove and refrigerator was the most difficult, production of those had slowed down dramatically during the war, and the demand from returning military people was tremendous. We also had to put our name on a list to buy a car and wait until one was available. I went to work for Southern Bell, in the same building that Noel's aunt worked, which was very fortunate. I was secretary in the personnel department, a job I kept for nine years.

Noel's uncle was also in the Army. When he returned home in late 1946, he and his wife moved to Jonesboro, Georgia. We were anxious to get settled somewhere so we bought a two acre lot next to them. With the help of his uncle, Noel designed a one bedroom home for us. The carpenter put up the house but we finished the inside ourselves. We settled into our first real home in early 1947. With both of us working in Atlanta, we formed a car pool to help cover expenses by providing transportation for other Jonesboro residents who worked downtown.

We had lived in our house one year when an ice storm knocked out the electricity and our furnace caught fire, burning the inside of the house. That was the first time I remember my father's words, *If that's the worst thing that can happen, I would be lucky.* We were lucky the city fire department got there before the house was totally destroyed.

This was when the citizens of Jonesboro gave us a helping hand that started us on the path of volunteering in the community. We had made plans to buy home insurance on Monday night, but we were one day late. So with no insurance, the group who built the house came by and said if we would pay for the lumber, they would put our home back the way it was. The upholstery company came by and picked up the furniture that needed recovery and just charged us for the material used. The cleaners came by to clean and refresh our clothes—at no charge. Within four weeks we were back in our home. We moved in and repainted the walls just like they had been.

We both joined the American Legion post and became involved in raising money for a Post home. I joined the Jonesboro chapter of the Georgia Federation of Women's Clubs. One of our projects was to start a library by gathering books from individuals and by using a vacant building to display them for people to check them out. Eventually our group joined the Flint River Library Chapter and the county built a building for the library. I served on the county library board for five years.

Joining the Women's Club gave me an opportunity to serve on several committees in my community. During this time, Jonesboro celebrated its 100th anniversary and the entire community helped to build a youth center, which is still in use.

A leisurely Seine River boat trip with friends – Summer 1945

Helen at home in Woonsocket, SD after the
war was over

Helen and Noel on their wedding day

Helen and Noel's first home, in Riverdale, GA, had five acres where they always had 10-15 Collies they were raising.

Helen adjusts Jon's seat belt – Seat Belt Safety campaign – 1960

Billboards like this one were common around Atlanta in the early 1960's.

MY LIFE SINCE WWII

To wrap up this book, I will breeze through the next forty or so years of my life and then spend a little more time on what I've done since my retirement from Delta Airlines at the age of 60. As I look back on my retirement years, I believe I may have some words of wisdom that the Baby Boomer generation may benefit from as they enter their retirement years.

In 1955 we were very fortunate to be able to adopt a five month old son, Noel Jonathan, Jr., which we called Jon. I immediately quit work to become a stay-at-home mom, while continuing to volunteer in the community with fund raising drives as well as club work. At one time I was State Chairman of the Safety Committee when our national program was to install seat belts in all cars. The first seat belt in Georgia was installed in my car, and we placed billboards all over the city of Atlanta and eventually all the cars got seatbelts.

As a hobby, Noel purchased a registered Collie and started showing him at all the local dog shows. It was the beginning of the Deep South Collie Kennel, where we raised puppies and showed the dogs nationally. Eventually he became a judge, not only locally, but nationally. We belonged to the local club and also the national club, serving on both boards.

In 1956, I was asked to be secretary and treasurer of the John Word West Educational Foundation. We sent ten boys and girls to a four-year college. They only had to pay back the initial amount, with no interest, after they had a job. They all paid it back eventually. John West was a retired college president of North Georgia College in Dahlonega, who was taught by Noel's grandfather, a veteran of the Civil War, as well as a teacher at a one-room school in Jonesboro. Colonel West operated the Fair of 1860 in Jonesboro, which was a museum of artifacts from that area and era. After he died, we sold the museum to a group of people from Columbus and it is now called Westville. The money we received from the sale was given in memory of the colonel to Clayton State and to Georgia Military School in College Park, Georgia.

We moved to Riverdale in 1957 where we had acreage to build a bigger kennel and have more space for the dogs. We were active in the local Lions Club and the Community Club, as well as the junior baseball organization.

Our son, Jon, started kindergarten in 1959 at St. John Catholic School in Hapeville. I was fortunate to be employed as secretary in the school office, which gave me the opportunity to have the same hours as he did. When he finished grade school, we enrolled him in Marist High School in Atlanta, in 1967.

That fall of 1967 I went to work for Delta Air Lines as a secretary in the maintenance base, a job I kept until 1982. We were very fortunate that it gave us the opportunity to travel. We took several trips to Europe to show Jon where we both served and experienced the wonders of Europe.

In 1982, the year I retired from Delta and expected a full life with my family, my life dramatically changed when I lost my entire family. Noel's aunt died on January 4, Jon died from a fire in his condo on February 22, Noel's uncle died on February 23, and Noel was in the hospital with a heart attack. On November 27, 1982, Noel died from another heart attack.

I was in shock and depression—no one should have to handle that much tragedy in such a short period of time. I felt like I was in the middle of the ocean, in a small boat with no land in sight, and with one paddle which was taking me around in circles. My faith and the power of prayer helped me to survive. I knew I had to do something to get out of my deep depression, so I decided to get into volunteer work.

I went to the local Red Cross office and asked for a volunteer assignment, which was helping with blood drives in the south Metro area. I served in different areas for 22 years, including receiving the Clara Barton Award for my service. It gave me the opportunity of encouraging others, including Delta retirees, to be a part of helping with the drives. They were local citizens giving back to the community in many ways. Delta used our group of Delta retirees to help in projects, including fund drives and many other ways, including refurbishing Ship

41, a vintage DC-3 (the civilian version of the C-47 planes I saw flying over London from which the paratroopers jumped on D-Day in 1944), and building the Delta museum. I served on the Delta museum board for many years and took part in the purchasing of the Spirit of Delta airplane, an L1011 bought for Delta by their employees.

Noel was treasurer of the Collie Club of America organization when he passed away. The board appointed me to fill the vacancy and re-elected me for several years until a foundation was established to fund grants to veterinarian colleges to research problems with all dogs, including Collies. I served first as treasurer and then president, and later on the board of directors of that foundation. I also had an opportunity to judge puppy matches at shows all over the country.

In 1994, on the 50th anniversary of D-Day, my life changed completely…

In 1994, my life changed completely after revealing that I was involved in the D-Day operation in WWII. Keeping the secret for 50 years was due to the intense training received by the FBI. They impressed upon me—and I'm sure the other girls—that if we disclosed any of the plans, we were putting our life in danger. The officers who were involved in our project also made me realize that we were under oath not to reveal anything that went on in that room in London fifty years earlier. Typing TOP SECRET at the top of every page meant what it said.

I was very hesitant when I told my friend, LeAnne Nix, that I was the one that typed the D-Day plans, but she felt the public needed to know and called the Atlanta Journal newspaper and a local TV station. And now you know the rest of the story.

After the story was published in the newspaper, officials at Fort Gillem invited me to speak at their D-Day program. That morning at 7:00 AM, the WSB radio program interviewed me over the phone. Then I received an invitation from the USO to attend a banquet at the Governor's Mansion with Governor Zell Miller and other guests. Another invitation came from the Canadian Embassy to be their guest, along with the French Ambassador, for a cocktail party at his home before the Governor's dinner. In was an honor to have my picture taken with both Ambassadors, as well as later with the Governor and his wife, along with a tour of the Governor's Mansion—what an impressive home. That was the beginning of my life, after I revealed my secret.

Invitations began to pour in from community organizations, civic groups, schools, military groups, church groups, etc. I had suddenly become a minor celebrity.

To be able to talk to school-children, from first grade to college was a challenge. I had to make my talk according to my audience. The younger children were told why I joined in words they could understand— patriotism, follow orders, respect my country and my flag. One child asked if I had been scared and another asked if it made me cry, and, of course, I told them yes. Older student questions were about what the history books said and what I saw. Military organizations were interested in the plans and how they were written. When talking to seniors in nursing homes or retirement homes, I realized that they had lived in my time so I asked them to tell me what they did during the war. It was very interesting to hear what they worked in—aircraft factory, or USO, or other means of supporting the war. I always impressed on them that they made sacrifices, just like the military did. All in all, it is a great education for me to meet so many wonderful people, of all ages, who are interested in The War.

In addition to the many speaking engagements, I was contacted by Bob Babcock, my co-author of this book, in 2003 to do a videotaped interview for the Veterans History Project. We stayed in touch and he had me speak at several events in support of that great project, where interviews are preserved forever in the Library of Congress.

My friend and companion, Terry Mock, made the arrangements for me to participate in the dedication of the World War II Memorial in Washington, DC on Memorial Day weekend in 2004. We flew to Dulles Airport and had hotel reservations at the Willard Hotel. The hotel manager greeted us and escorted us to a suite—the beginning of a wonderful weekend. We were close enough to walk to the Memorial and enjoyed a leisurely stroll, reading all the inscriptions and meeting other visitors on Friday. We enjoyed a luncheon at the Women's Memorial and saw all their displays as well as taking a tour through Arlington National Cemetery. Saturday morning we joined the long line of visitors to hear the speakers, including President Bush. Sunday we covered the mall and enjoyed the many interesting exhibits that had been set up in honor of this occasion. Returning home late that evening, we were tired but very happy we had been able to attend such a historic celebration.

In October, 2008, I was invited to take an Honor Flight again to Washington, DC to visit the WWII Memorial. The flight was definitely an honor. We assembled in the Methodist Church in Fayetteville at 6:00 am to enjoy a good breakfast and listen to some WWII era music from one of the local bands. We received a rousing send-off by the Honor Flight committee and boarded buses with a police honor guard for the airport. Walking through the airport, we were greeted by cheers from spectators, something we did not receive when we returned from service at the end of WWII. It was very heartwarming. The same kind of greeting was given us when we disembarked from the flight in Washington. A group of escorts, with wheel chairs for those who needed them, met our flight and accompanied us all day long, taking care of anything we needed. A bus took us to the WWII Memorial where we enjoyed a very leisurely morning with time to look at whatever we wanted and to spend as much time as we desired. A box lunch was provided as we boarded the buses to tour other highlights—the Vietnam Wall, the Korean War Memorial, the Iwo Jima statue, and Arlington National Cemetery. When we arrived back in Fayetteville, escorted again by a police honor guard, at 1:00 am the next morning, we were very tired but very appreciative of the tremendous effort the Honor Flight Group had extended to us.

Thirty Years of Volunteering After I Retired from Delta

I retired from Delta at age sixty, thinking we would have many years of traveling. But losing my family that year changed my life completely.

As a Delta retiree, I was elected secretary of the organization of retirees. The group was used in many capacities. We handled distribution of publications, blood drives, community activities for the company, and whatever projects that were needed. As a group we traveled all over the United States as well as several tours of Europe.

Volunteering at the military lounge sponsored by Delta Airlines was another opportunity for the retirees to make a difference. For 17 years we gave our time over the Christmas and New Year's holidays to not only welcome the military as they passed through the Atlanta airport, but to serve them food and drinks. I usually took the 3:00 am time slot when the first busload of soldiers arrived from the bases outside of Atlanta, headed home for the holidays. Home-baked treats were provided by employees as well as retirees. It was a very rewarding project for everyone. We stopped those efforts when the USO took up a permanent presence at the Atlanta airport, a job they continue to do to every day of the year. As their motto says, the USO will be there "until they all come home."

When the Collie Club of America elected me to fill the treasurer's office that Noel had held, it gave me the opportunity to attend dog shows all over the country and judge puppy classes. I received the Right Stuff Award, Meritorious Award, and was elected a member of a research foundation for Collies.

Helen's work with the Collie Club of America was described in the following speech as she was awarded the Right Stuff Award:

The last Outstanding Service Award is very dear to me. For just a few short years ago, I stood up here and did a eulogy to this lady's husband and our best friend in collies. And, so it is that we would have to consider her our second best friend. And this award tonight is unique also as this gal has played a secondary role for many years. For, you see, the collies were her husband's hobby. Oh, I'm not saying that she had nothing to do with them. Far from it. She helped with the kennel chores, typed the letters, cooked for the groups that came to visit, and gave unflinching support to her husband. And then, on show days, she would go shopping. But when her husband died, she said to me, "Ted, the family and the friends were thoughtful and nice, but it was the collie folks that came to my rescue and stayed in my heart."

What qualifies her for this award, you say? She jumped in and handled the treasurer's job flawlessly for several years now. But, of more importance, she has taken her unlimited Delta Airlines pass and has become the Collie Club of America's traveling "get it done gal." Whenever there is a problem, this gal piles on the airplane and off she goes in her very quiet, very competent, let's get it done manner. Ladies and gentlemen, she shall appreciate a grand and glorious welcome from you, and what a glorious lady she is, our dear friend, let's hear it for Helen Denton.

(Sustained applause).

Today, I am heavily involved in Veterans of Foreign Wars activities. I have served on the board of my local chapter for several years. When I was commander of my post, we were recognized by the city of Riverdale for planting a tree to remember WWII veterans. We built on that start by planting a tree for the Korean War and Vietnam War veterans in the City Park. We also researched the names of fallen veterans from all wars and engraved their name on a monument at the city square, as well as building a walkway of bricks with names of veterans. Each year we place a flag on the graves of veterans in both the Methodist and Baptist cemeteries on Memorial Day. For several years we have sponsored a Veterans parade on Veterans Day.

Speaking at schools has been another honor that has meant a lot to me. Several have been outstanding, such as the JC Booth School in Fayetteville where I have been invited back several times. In 2011 I spoke twice to an assembly of 250 students, a total of 500 students who heard the story of my WWII experiences. This was especially of interest to me since this was the school that had their students write a personal letter to each veteran who took an Honor Flight trip to Washington, DC. I had the opportunity to personally meet the young student who wrote to me—Marguerite Stoner.

Another outstanding school was Newnan High School. For several years they invited veterans from all the wars to meet the students, one class at a time, in a National Guard auditorium where the veterans displayed their memorabilia on a table. Each student had the opportunity to interview a veteran. They also teach a class on WWII where I would spend the day talking to each class. They asked very intelligent questions to verify what they read in their history books.

Some of the schools were elementary schools where I would speak about patriotism, getting along with different people, finishing a project assigned, and respect for our flag.

Other groups that have invited me to speak are church and community organizations. These are mostly people who have retired. It gives me an opportunity to encourage them to volunteer to make their retirement lives meaningful. There are so many organizations that need help and are just waiting for someone to volunteer. I've learned that when you give of your time and your talent, you gain a feeling of being needed and are helping someone who appreciates your effort. As I said at the opening of this section, having lost my family the same year that I retired, I couldn't have survived and thrived without my involvement in volunteer activities. I encourage all retirees reading this to get out of their comfort zone and volunteer—our country needs us to continue to set the example for them.

I will wrap up with a story about an honor I received at the 110th Veterans of Foreign Wars convention in Phoenix, Arizona on August 16-18, 2009.

I am a member of VFW Post #3650 in Riverdale, GA. My commander, Ronald Stubbs, and I left Hartsfield-Jackson International Airport in Atlanta on Delta flight 1025 at 8:50 a.m. on Sunday, August 16, a three-hour flight to Phoenix, Arizona, arriving at 9:52 a.m. We were met at the baggage area by Mr. Jerry Manor, Deputy Director, National Veterans Service, who escorted us to curbside where a car was waiting to take us to the Hyatt Regency Hotel where we had already been checked in.

We unpacked our bags and met in the lobby of the hotel and proceeded to the Phoenix International Convention Center where we registered and received our credentials and security badge. We acclimated ourselves to the assembly hall and then returned to the hotel to meet with other delegates from Georgia. By that time it was 6:00 p.m., 9:00 p.m. in Atlanta, and I was ready to call it a day.

Monday morning we were met in the lobby after breakfast by Dawn Jirak. I was also escorted by two George State troopers who had provided transportation for Ronald Keller of the Georgia State inspector's office. These two troopers were my constant companions, which was a big help passing through the hundreds of protestors outside the Center. Some were in protest of and some were supporting President Obama being there. We had to pass through security where they examined my credentials and inspected my person and bags. We then proceeded to the special seating arrangements made for those of us who would have their picture taken with the President.

When my turn came, I was motioned by the deputy director to follow him to the designated area, accompanied by the troopers. We were in a very secure area where the President was standing with the photographer. President Obama smiled at me, took my hands, and said, "I know all about you, Mrs. Denton, that you are a WWII veteran who served under General Eisenhower in London and typed the battle plans for the D-Day invasion." I said, "Yes, Sir." Then he commented on how young I looked for a WWII veteran. I replied, "I came from good genes." He said he wanted this photo to be special so he put his arms around me and pulled me close and the photo was taken. I told him that I prayed for him every night. He replied that he needed it. I then left the room and followed the troopers up on the stage where the President would be speaking.

President Obama entered the stage and proceeded to the podium and began by recognizing the Governor of Arizona, the Mayor of Phoenix, several Congressmen, and then he said, "I would like to recognize Mrs. Helen Kogel Denton, a World War II veteran who served in Europe under General Eisenhower and typed the battle plans for the invasion of France." He turned to me and I stood up and received a standing ovation from over 3,000 veterans. Camera from TV stations and newspapers went off like a Fourth of July celebration. I was so surprised to be recognized in front of the assembly. When he finished his address, he turned to leave the podium and stopped in front of me, took my hands, and kissed my cheek. Again the flashbulbs exploded. Again I was overwhelmed but so proud to be recognized again.

When we had the first break from the program after the President left the auditorium, I motioned to the troopers that I was ready to return to the hotel. On arriving we joined a large Georgia delegation of veterans. I received many exciting comments from my comrades on the special attention of the President. By 6:00 p.m. Phoenix time, 9:00 p.m. Atlanta time, I was ready to call it a day. An interesting side note, as the President left the podium, he left his water glass, untouched, on the table. His assistants asked if I would like to have it. His Presidential seal was on the cover of the glass. I drank the water and kept the glass as a souvenir.

Tuesday morning, August 18, I rose at 5:30 a.m., dressed and proceeded to the lobby, checked out, and met the troopers by 6:30 a.m. I had been invited to a Veterans' Women's Breakfast in another part of the center. I was completely exhausted when we arrived, it was much further than I had expected. I stayed until 7:00 a.m. when I motioned for the troopers that I had to be in another part of the Center for the presentation of the Commander's Award. They had secured a wheelchair for me to use the rest of the day.

I was one of several people escorted to the stage, with the troopers close by. At approximately 10:00 a.m., VFW Commander-in-Chief Glen M. Gardner presented me with the Gold Medal of Merit Award and citation. This award is presented to individuals to recognize exceptional service rendered to their country, community, and mankind on a national and international level. He read a very lengthy report on all my volunteer activities in the community as well as my service as a VFW member and years as the Commander of Post 3650 in Riverdale.

He placed a gold medallion around my neck, gave me a framed certificate of merit, and gave me time to make a comment. I thanked him for the honor and mentioned that I was born and raised on a farm in South Dakota (which brought a clap from their delegates), attended college in Minnesota where I entered the service. Noel and I lived in Jonesboro when we first married and that is where I started my community volunteer services. Later we had moved to Riverdale. It wasn't until America and the world celebrated the 50th anniversary of D-Day that I first told anyone that I had served under General Eisenhower and had typed the D-Day battle plans. I joined VFW Post 3650 and now spend my time visiting schools and many organizations. With school children I stress patriotism and what it means to be a Veteran. To civic organizations, I make sure I thank those who made so much sacrificing at home to support the war effort.

By this time it was noon. The troopers escorted me back to the hotel and, along with Commander Stubbs we had lunch. Mr. Manor was waiting for us in the lobby of the hotel. I said goodbye to the troopers, thanked Mr. Manor for his assistance, and his driver took the two of us to the airport for our return to Atlanta, arriving at 9:40 p.m., two very tired travelers who had enjoyed a wonderful time.

Noel with his favorite collie, Jeremiah, taken shortly before his death

Helen with Lassie – they rode first class on Delta from California to Atlanta

Noel, Jon, Helen - taken the fall before Jon died

Local volunteers honored for outstanding Red Cross service

30 years of service honored at annual meeting

Two Fayette County residents have been honored for outstanding volunteer work with the Metropolitan Atlanta Chapter of the American Red Cross.

Georgia Knight, a Fayetteville resident and an American Red Cross volunteer since the 1960s, was honored by the chapter as the recipient of the Charles C. Rice Award, given annually to an individual for extraordinary service in the area of Red Cross safety. Helen Denton, a Red Cross volunteer since 1982, was honored as Blood Volunteer of the Year.

Beginning her volunteering for the Red Cross in high school by working at the local hospital and teaching water safety classes, Knight has remained a volunteer for more than 30 years.

She started volunteering with the South Metro Service Center in Morrow in 1993 in the areas of blood drives, First Aid Stations and CPR/first aid instructor. Since then she has trained more than 300 people in CPR/first aid.

Knight knows personally the importance of knowing CPR. Her own father suffered a heart attack several years ago.

"Because I knew CPR, I was able to use it on my dad, and even though he didn't make it, I knew I had done everything that I could," she explained. "I can't imagine what it would have been like to stand there and do nothing and always wonder if it would have made a difference. I hope by teaching CPR that it might help someone else be there for a loved one or friend when they need them."

In addition to her hours spent volunteering at the Red Cross Center, Knight is active at the Fayetteville Community Hospital. A career teacher, she is involved in the hospital's summer youth program, training youth in CPR and has been instrumental in initiating courses in CPR/first aid and babysitting at the hospital.

Knight has taught at the annual free Red Cross CPR Saturday for seven years and trained more than

Georgia Knight, left, with Helen Denton. Photo/Special.

200 youths in programs such as Safe on My Own, a program that offers children instruction on how to be safe when at home as well as Whales Tales, a program designed to teach elementary school age children water safety rules. She also teaches first aid at the Red Cross Elementary Leadership Development Conference taught annually in Fayette County.

Since 1998, Knight has been a volunteer orientation trainer as well as a member of the Red Cross Disaster Action Team. Currently, she serves as a member of South Metro Service Center's volunteer cabinet, speaker's bureau and also volunteers at the Hope House, a care center for terminally ill children.

For the past 18 years, Denton has been a valuable asset in getting Delta Airlines, one of Atlanta's biggest corporations, to donate much needed blood four times a year, said a Red Cross spokesman. Being the coordinator of Delta's blood drives has provided Denton with many volunteer hours and the local blood banks with more than 50,000 pints of blood.

When she retired from Delta in

1982, Denton became a Red Cross volunteer and now helps to recruit, train and assign 250 people each year to work blood drives in Atlanta. From 1997-1999 alone, she volunteered more than 1,000 hours each year as blood drive coordinator, recruiter and speaker.

"Helen has been a tremendous asset in the South Metro Service Center blood drives," said Ruben Brown, South Metro Service Center director. "She has been instrumental in schools and teaching the importance of giving blood to those who need it most."

This is not the first time that Denton's outstanding work has gained recognition from the community. She has been honored with several other service awards including the Clara Barton Award of Meritorious Service, United Way Community Service award and the Martin Luther King Jr. Center for Nonviolent Social Change Inc. award.

Still, apart from all these honors, Denton maintains a simple philosophy about her community service. "You receive much more than you give," she said. "And if you reach out, there is always someone to help you."

Five years after retirement from Delta, Helen regularly took the Christmas Eve shift at the Delta military hospitality room, greeting troops passing through the Atlanta airport. This job is now handled on a daily basis by USO Georgia.

Helen with Georgia Governor Zell Miller and his wife at the USO Georgia banquet on the 50th anniversary of D-Day, June 6, 1994. It was at this time when Helen started talking about her role in World War II.

As a Delta Museum volunteer, Helen was on the inaugural flight of the restored DC-3 that is still in the Delta Museum in Atlanta.

As a long time Delta retiree and volunteer, Helen receives a lifetime achievement volunteer award from the president of Delta Air Lines.

Helen at Lake City Elementary - November 2009

Officers of Delta Retirees
in 1982

Helen Denton standing in front of
Helen Denton Street sign

BELOW: Parade on Veterans
Day 2008 when Helen Denton
Street was named.

Helen receives an appreciation award
from Georgia Governor Sonny Perdue.

Helen poses with the Noel Denton
Best of Breed Collie Award

Each Memorial Day, Helen participates with her VFW post to put flags on veterans graves in local cemeteries

Helen regularly speaks at schools – here she is with students of J.C. Boothe School

Helen poses with Pati Merrell, President
of the Collie Club of America as she
received a lifetime achievement award

Helen and her closest friend, Terry Mock, participated in the
WWII Memorial Dedication in Washington, DC in May 2004

FROM

TO: Ms. Helen Denton

Marguerite Stonier

(CENSOR'S STAMP)   SEE INSTRUCTION NO. 2   (Sender's complete address above)

Dear Ms. Denton,
          Thank you for serving in WW II. I know it must have been hard leaving your friends, family, and your home. Everyone in my class appericates what you did back in 1940-1945. Although, Mrs. Springer (our Soical Studies teacher) has not yet taught us about WW II, we will learn about it soon enough

          Here are just a few questions. What did you do when you in the military? What branch were you in? Where were you stationed? What rank were you? When you vollenteered did you come out of college?

          My mom served in the Army for 26 years as a sergeant 1st class. My dad served also served as a Marine and Solider. for 15 years. He started as a Lieutenant. They are retired now. I hope you enjoy your trip to the WW II Memorial.

          Here's just a little about me. I'm a student at Huddleston Elementary. I'm in the 6th grade. My favorite subject is Soical Studies, Science, and Writing. I'm eleven years old. My birthday was September 20th. Again Hope you enjoy the Memorial.

                                        Sincerely,
                                        Marguerite S.

Helen was presented the VFW Commander-in-Chief Gold Medal of Merit award at the VFW National Convention in Phoenix, AZ in 2009. President Barack Obama congratulates her.

Many times Helen has been asked if she had a picture taken with General Eisenhower. Her immediate response is always, "Corporals don't ask generals to have their picture taken with them." To alleviate that, at a North Georgia Veterans meeting in September 2012, Helen had this picture taken with LTG (Ret) Steve Arnold (left) and MG (Ret) Phil Anderson (right).

LeAnne Nix and Helen Denton - LeAnne is the one who convinced Helen, in 1994, that her significant role in WWII needed to be told to the world.

ABOUT THE AUTHOR

Helen was born and raised on a farm that was homesteaded by her father and grandfather in South Dakota. She finished a two year business college course before she joined the Women's Auxiliary Army Corps, which later became the Women's Army Corps, in early 1943.

She served in the European theater from January 1944 to October 1945 under General Eisenhower's command, serving on his staff.

Helen retired from Delta Airlines in April 1982 and has been volunteering ever since with the American Red Cross, Delta Pioneers, is past commander of VFW Post 3650, and continues to work in many additional volunteer capacities—including meeting regularly with school children and civic, military, and other groups—always speaking about patriotism and volunteerism.

APPENDIX—Operation Overlord as typed by Helen Denton, this is an extract, not the full extent of the work Helen did for the Operation Overlord orders. This is not the copy Helen typed. It has been retyped by historians for use on the internet.

[8-3.4 AA Volume 7]

OUTLINE OF OPERATION OVERLORD

[Note: This manuscript was prepared by the Historical Section of the G-4 of the Communications Zone, European Theater of Operations (COMZ, ETOUSA) as volume seven of its multi-volume manuscript organizational history. It was subsequently deposited at the Office of the Chief of Military History (OCMH; now US Army Center of Military History) for reference use by historians preparing the official history of the Army in World War II. It is typical of the kinds of detailed studies routinely acquired (as in this case) or carried out by the deployed historians during World War II. The original is on file in the Historical Manuscripts Collection (HMC) under file number 8-3.4 AA v.7, which should be cited in footnotes, along with the title. It is reproduced here with only those limited modifications required to adapt to the World Wide Web; spelling, punctuation, and slang usage have not been altered from the original. Where modern explanatory notes were required, they have been inserted as italicized text in square brackets.]

SECTION VII

OUTLINE OF OPERATION OVERLORD

PART I: OUTLINE OF OPERATION OVERLORD
TAB I: OUTLINE OF TACTICAL PROBLEM

1. OBJECT—The ultimate mission of the Commanding General, ETOUSA, is the total defeat of Germany. The object of Operation OVERLORD is to mount and carry out an operation with forces and equipment established in the United Kingdom and with target date as designated, to secure a lodgement area on the Continent from which further offensive operations can be developed. This will be part of a concerted assault upon German occupied Europe from the United Kingdom, the Mediterranean and Russia.

2. <u>GENERAL INFORMATION</u>—The operation will be executed in two phases:

<u>Phase I</u>—The assault and capture of an initial lodgement area, including the development of airfield sites in the CAEN area and the capture of CHERBOURG.

<u>Phase II</u>—Enlargement of the area captured in Phase I, to include the Brittany peninsula, all ports south to the Loire (inclusive) and the area between the Loire and the Seine.

Phase I and some parts of Phase II will be executed by U.S., British and Canadian Forces assigned or attached to 21st Army Group.

At a time to be designated by the Supreme Commander, the First U.S. Army Group, as such, will take over certain areas, missions and U.S. Forces then under 21st Army Group.

3. <u>ALLIED FORCES AVAILABLE</u>—On the target date it is estimated that there will be available in United Kingdom:

<u>Land Forces</u>—21 U.S. divisions (13 Infantry, 6 Armored, and 2 Airborne), 17 British divisions (10 Infantry, 5 Armored, and 2 Airborne) and supporting troops of both Forces.

<u>Air Forces</u>—331 U.S. Squadrons (214 in Eighth [Strategic] Air Force, and 117 in Ninth [Tactical] Air Force) and 220 British Squadrons. Figures for each Air Force include squadrons of all types.*

4. <u>MAJOR CONDITIONS AFFECTING THE SUCCESS OF THE OPERATION</u>

An operation of the nature and. size of operation OVERLORD has never previously been attempted in history. It is fraught with hazards, both in nature and magnitude which to not obtain in any other theater of the present world war. In order that the operation may have a reasonable prospect of success, it is assumed that certain conditions must exist concerning the major obstacles. These conditions are:

<u>German Fighter Strength</u>—There will be an overall reduction in the German fighter force to ensure necessary air superiority. Recent figures

on destruction of German fighter production capacity and of fighters themselves in aerial combat are encouraging; however, it must be remembered that the effort of the German Air Force on the target date need not be sustained as the battle for the lodgement area will be won or lost in the first few days.

Coast Defense - The German Coast Defense has been designed primarily to delay access to principal ports. Our landing will be made presumably in a lightly defended area as the Germans consider a landing there likely to be unsuccessful because of its distance from a major port.

German Land Forces—The German defense policy is to defeat any attempted invasion of France and the Low Countries on the coasts. Offensive reserves are accordingly located within striking distance of the most vulnerable parts. It is assumed that, on D Day, German divisions in reserve will be so located that the number of first-quality divisions which could be deployed in the CAEN area to support the divisions

holding the coast should not exceed three divisions on D-Day, five divisions by D+2, or nine divisions by D+8.

PLANES: *Fighters - 2700; Hv Bombers - 1956; Med Bombers 456; Lt Bombers - 171; Photo Recon - 128; Plus Reserves.

Surprise—Though it should be possible to affect a considerable measure of tactical surprise, it will be impossible to achieve strategical surprise. Every effort must be made to draw the enemy's attention to our most favorable landing place, Pas de Calais, and away from our actual landing point, the CAEN area.

Beach Maintenance—Maintenance over beaches is a paramount in this amphibious operation. It is calculated that making full use of every captured port, large and small, 18 divisions must be maintained over beaches during the first month of operations, 12 divisions during the second month, and a number rapidly diminishing to NIL during the third month. Therefore, it is imperative that adequate measures be taken to provide sheltered waterways by artificial means, facilities on captured beaches for landing of vehicles and for the repair of damage to the beaches themselves by continual grounding of craft.

4. THE ASSAULT—The plan for the initial landing is based on two main principles—concentration of force and tactical surprise. Three Regimental Combat Teams of the First U.S. Army on the right, and five Brigade Groups of the British Second Army on the left, along with supporting air and naval forces, will make the assault in the CAEN area. The assault will be supported by airborne divisions. This will be followed by the early capture and development of airfield sites and the capture of the port of CHERBOURG, which will complete Phase I of the Operation.

It is these early days of the operation that will spell success or failure. Here is the race between the build-up of forces and supplies by Allied Forces and the bringing up of reserves by the Germans.

5. PHASE II -

First Army—After capturing CHERBOURG, and with its left flank protected by the British Second Army, the first U.S. Army will drive to the south and southeast to cut the

Brittany Peninsula and secure the ports of NANTES and ST. NAZAIRE. One Corps will turn west to clear up the peninsula.

Then, First Army will advance the line of the Upper Seine prepared for further action to the northeast.

Third Army—Third Army will land on the continent as soon as possible after First Army, probably about D+35-D+45 and will capture the Brittany peninsula and open the Brittany ports, unless this has already been done by First Army. After clearing the Brittany peninsular Third Army will concentrate on the right of the First Army, prepared to operate to the east, either in close conjunction with First Army or by swinging south of the Loire if a wider envelopment is feasible.

Situation on D+90—By D+90, occupation of the lodgment area is complete. U.S. and British Forces are on the Seine River, First and Third Armies are abreast, and First Army Group has been established as has a Communications line. Our forces are prepared for further offensive operations.

Situation maps showing the various stages of the capture of the lodgement area are attached.

6. <u>THE BUILD-UP OF US FORCES</u>—The anticipated build-up of U.S. Forces on the Continent is:

	F.F. & SOS		AIR FORCES		TOTAL	
	Veh	**Per**	**Veh**	**Per**	**Veh**	**Per**
D	9,456	89,750	146	707	9,602	90,467
D+5	27,758	188,000	1,804	9,542	29,562	197,542
D+15	66,882	385,500	5,190	25,147	72,072	410,747
D+30	120,057	660,000	11,355	56, 640	131,412	716,640
D+50	165,648	873,350	17,892	94,160	183,540	967,510
D+70	191,066	987,750	25,394	121,960	216,460	1,109,710
D+90	215,570	1,99,790	32,890	142,700	248,460	1,242,490

7. As stated previously, this operation is fraught with hazards. Unless these hazards are squarely faced and adequately overcome, the operation cannot succeed. There is no reason why they should not be overcome, provided the energies of all concerned are bent to the problem.

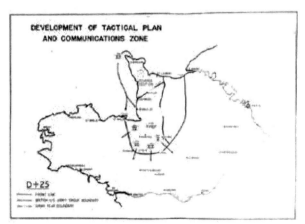

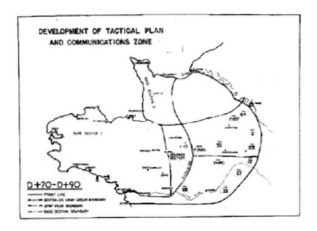

PART I: <u>OUTLINE OF OPERATION OVERLORD</u>
TAB 2a: <u>U.S. Artificial Harbor MULBERRY A</u>

<u>MULBERRY A</u> is the code name for the United States project for the building of an artificial harbor. Plans call for the construction of this artificial harbor at a beach on the French coast "extending from L 0° 54' 15" W, to O° 50' 30" W. The line of the beach runs 298° True. The towns of Vierville, St, Laurent-sur-Mer and Coleville are located in the rear of this area. (Port "MULBERRY" - Information, p. 1.)

The object of MULBERRY A is to provide an all-weather harbor so that a minimum of 5,000 long tons of stores, plus 1,000 vehicles and equipment, may be discharged per day.

Since the approval of the Project, vast quantities of British civilian labor have been employed in the construction, and large numbers of Army and Navy personnel engaged in portions of the final assembly of the various units.

As the project now stands, 12 block ships of approximately 400 ft each in length will be sunk in a line on the east are of the beach forming a GOOSEBERRY or small sheltered anchorage. At the same time, the west breakwater, formed of 8 PHOENIXES in a line, will be sunk to form the beginning of the west side of MULBERRY. PHOENIXES are reinforced concrete caissons, the largest of which is 204 ft long, 60 ft high and 60 ft wide. The seaward side of MULBERRY will be formed by sinking 34 PHOENIXs in a line, which will complete the inner shelter of MULBERRY A. These gigantic structures have a draft of 19 ft. and have a total displacement of 6,000 tons. The PHOENIXs are built with scow ends and equipped with all necessary appurtences *[sic]* for towing and valves for sinking.

48 BOMBARDONS, which are steel cruciform lilos, each 200 ft long, will be anchored to concrete blocks and located in two parallel lines about 800 ft apart to form a breakwater, 1,100 ft from the outer breakwater of PHOENIXES.

Within the west breakwater four LOBNITZ PIERHEADS with three causeways, each 1 mile long, will be locates to discharge vehicles and equipment, The west causeway will have a capacity of 40 tons, and each of the other two 25 tons capacity. LOBNITZ PIERHEADS, or spud pierheads are all-steel, watertight compartmented barges, 200 ft long, 60 ft wide, and have a draft of 10 ft and displace about 1,000 tons. The spuds themselves are all steel, and raised by electrically controlled winches which are capable of lifting the pierheads off floatation. The spud pierheads can accommodate three LST's and one coaster, each 325 ft, and five LCT's 100 ft each, simultaneously for discharge.

Inside the shelter provided by the 34 PHOENIXES, anchorage is obtained for seven Liberty ships (450 ft), five large coasters (300 ft), five medium coasters (275 ft) and seven small coasters and craft (150 to 200 ft).

The protection afforded by the entire MULBERRY project covers 21 miles of beach. As added insurance in discharge, forty 1,000 tons capacity barges have been ordered, and are now being delivered to the UK, which will be beached at high water mark and allowed to remain until unloaded.

RHINO FERRIES will be used in large numbers to discharge from coasters to beaches directly. RHINO FERRIES are 500 ton capacity barges made by assembling pontoons into a craft 175 ft long and 43 ft wide, powered by two pontoon barges, one on either side of the stern of the RHINO FERRY, each having an outboard and inboard propulsion unit.

DUKWs, PEEPS, LCTs, LBVs, and other small craft will be used in unprecedented numbers to assist in the discharge of stores from larger craft.*

NOTE: * Unfavorable weather conditions on 19 June 1944 marked the beginning of a severe storm which prevented the discharge of cargo for three successive days. Damage to the artificial port of MULBERRY A prevented its use for future operations. (FUSA, Report of Operations, 20 October 1943-1 August 1944, Book I, p. 78)

PART I: OUTLINE OF OPERATION OVERLORD
TAB 2b: SPECIAL PROBLEM—CONTINENTAL TRANSPORTATION

The Transportation Corps problem on the continent is principally one of adequate port capacity and of adequate motor transport facilities. The plans for build-up during the first 90 days call for a flow of 1,200,000. Tonnage requirements vary almost directly with the proposed build-up. For a maximum build-up basis, the planned activation and phasing of troops for ETOUSA will meet the problems with difficulty.

Tonnage requirements estimated depending upon the troop flow contemplated, can be accommodated by port and beach capacity by D plus 90. Sufficient port handling equipment, including barges, DUKWs and cranes should be on hand to meet the load with the exception of DUKWs, of which there is an apparent shortage of 5 companies. There is an apparent shortage of 16 port battalions, if each of the ports is to be used to its maximum estimated capacity, insofar as port stevedore labor is concerned, considering the mounting requirements in the UK.

Although port capacity may be adequate to receive tonnage requirements, the highway network will not in all cases permit the clearance and forwarding of the large tonnages required. This pertains particularly in the Cotentin peninsula where the combined capacity of beaches, minor ports and major ports exceed the road capacity to the south. If reserve tonnages are largely held in storage until rail capacity is developed, the road limitations may not prove to be insurmountable difficulties.

For the period up to D plus 90 no material reliance has been placed on railroad operation. Supply along the L/C for this period is planned by motor truck, with the exception of the relief that may be afforded by POL pipelines. It is planned to equip two-thirds of the available SOS Truck Companies (151 companies) with heavy equipment (truck-tractors and semi-trailers and other heavy equipment ordered on Ordnance Projects). If all equipment were to materialize as requested, there would still be an apparent appreciable shortage of truck companies if a maximum troop flow were to be used. This obstacle may possibly be alleviated by SOS employment of truck companies of the second and third armies to enter the continent, provided adequate drivers could be obtained to permit 24 hour operation.

Provided rail operation begins by D plus 60 rather than the conservative estimate of D plus 90, and provided heavy vehicular project equipment is made available in time for the critical period from D to D plus 90, it is estimated that the transportation system will be effective.

Present plans for railroad reconstruction and operation call for two general lines of communication, one running from Cherbourg south through the Cotentin peninsula through Lison and terminating in the Rennes (main supply) area, and the other running north from St. Nazaire to the same area. These two lines are first US priority construction. Second priority, and to be accomplished by D plus 90 includes the link from St. Nazaire to Le Mans and from Rennes to Le Mans.*

NOTE: * During the period D+90 to D+360 plans provided for the development of four principal Lines of Communication:

> (1) Quiberon - Rennes - Le Mans - Paris;
>
> (2) St. Nazaire - Nantes - Tour - Orleans - Paris;
>
> (3) Cherbourg - Laigle - Paris;
>
> (4) Le Havre and Dieppe - Chauny.

Plans called for the extension of the rail lines which connect base ports with the forward areas. The extension of double track on the Le Mans-Paris line, double tracking the line from Surdon-Laigle to Paris, and the reconstruction of the double track line along the Loire Valley to Paris route, were among the important rail construction projects contemplated. When the British transferred the control of the Le Havre and Dieppe-Chauny line to the Americans, it was planned to extend the first three lines referred to above so that they would connect with this fourth line of communication. (Hq ETOUSA, AG 400.312, 8 June 1944, Planning Directive Series "H" #3, Subject: Projects for Continental Operations (PROCO), D+91 to D+ 360, to Chiefs of Supply Services, ETOUSA, p. 5).

PART I: <u>OUTLINE OF OPERATION OVERLORD</u>
TAB 2c: <u>SPECIAL PROBLEM - PORTS</u>

Studies have been made by ETOUSA considering reconstruction and development of fifteen (15) ports which include Brest, Cherbourg, Granville, Concarneau, La Pallice, St. Brieue, Lorient, St. Nazaire, Nantes, La Rochelle, Morlaix, L'Abervrach, St. Malo, Les Sables D'Olenne and Bordeaux. In the ports under consideration tide range is excessive, amounting in some cases to as much as 45 feet. Large scale engineering works have been necessary in the construction of locked basins to overcome this physical draw-back, and to permit accommodation of large ships. In many ports constant dredging is required to maintain navigable channels. Port operations under normal conditions are not simple. After capture, operation will depend on such facilities as can be provided through rapid repair and improvised structures for the discharge of military cargoes, either from large vessels direct to reconstructed quays, or by use of coasters, lighters, and DUKWs.

From reconnaissance it is assumed that every effort will be made to destroy each port and its facilities by mining approaches, blocking approaches, destruction of facilities, destruction of railway roads and bridges, and destruction of locks. Allied air attacks have been heavy on all ports. For example, at St. Nazaire at the present time not a building of the entire Chantiers de Penhouet has escaped damage and the basin quays have suffered to the point where they are unusable by merchant ships. Dredging has almost ceased. It is estimated that, when the enemy has evacuated, the ports will be from 75% to 90% destroyed.

Plans call for the initial capture of Cherbourg which is designated as a U.S. Port with a British sub-area allocation. Operations are scheduled to begin by D+11. Clearance of British supplies from the decks to the British transit area near the port will be a U.S. responsibility with the use of U.S. transport and labor units as long as U.S. facilities suffice. When this is no longer possible, port authorities will notify 21st Army Group which will assign British transport and labor units necessary to supplement U.S. resources. The British transit area is to be staffed by British personnel. Other ports will be developed and operated by the Ally capturing them.*

* Fwd Ech Com Z Plan, Annex 13, Transportation Corps Plan, 10 May 1944, p. 1.

First U.S. Army plans to phase in personnel, supplies equipment and vehicles over the beaches of Quineville, St. Laurent and Madeleine on D-Day, through the port of Isigny on D+7, the artificial port of St. Laurent on D+12, Grandcamp on D+14 and St. Vaast on D+21. Barfleur is scheduled to open by D+20, Granville on D+24, St. Malo D+27, Brest and Rade de Brest D+53, Quiberon Bay D+54 and Lorient D+57.*

* Fwd Ech, ComZ Plan, Annex 13, Transportation Corps Plan, 10 May 1944, p. 2, 3, 5, 8.

Build-up previously cited, requires 40,000 tons/day by D+90 which will have to be maintained in order to build up reserves and provide maintenance. 15,000 tons/day is maximum capacity for UK ports (outloading)—25,000 tons/day required ex US.*

NOTE: *Port Capacity on D+90 was estimated at 45,950 long tons in comparison to the estimated tonnage flow of 37,500 tons. Tonnages were expected to increase to the point where they exceeded port capacities between D+120 and D+150, unless Nantes and St. Nazaire were captured and placed in operation during the interval, and unless the capacities of the ports in operation were increased. Com Z expected an increase in port capacity with the anticipated transfer of the British Mulberry at Arromanches and the port of Caen to the U.S. Army by D+210. No additional increase was contemplated until D+300 when the British were expected to withdraw from Le Havre, Fecamp, and Dieppe. Invasion preplanning did not include plans for the opening and operation of any additional French ports south of Nantes. Facilities available at La Pallice, Rochefort and Bordeaux should not be developed unless future operations disclosed the necessity for such action. (Hq ETOUSA, AG 400.312, 8 June 1944, Planning Directive, Series H #3, Subj: Projects for Continental Operations (PROCO), D+91 to D+360, to Chiefs of Supply Services, ETOUSA, p.5.)

PART I: OUTLINE OF OPERATION OVERLORD
TAB 2d: SPECIAL PROBLEM

1. RAILWAY, ROAD AND BRIDGING CONSTRUCTION

By D+90 it will be necessary to construct 425 miles of main line railway. By D+240, construction of 1,325 miles will have to be completed. A detailed study has been made of all railway lines using Intelligence Reports from US and British sources, coordinated with aerial photographs. From these data, it is estimated that 40 lineal foot of bridging per mile of track and 5.6 lineal feet of culvert per mile of track trill be required. In view of enemy methods and technique in demolition, it is estimated that over 95% of track and bridges will be destroyed between D and D+90. About 30% of the track will be recoverable; none of the destroyed bridges will be recoverable before D+90; and only about 10% thereafter.

Based on this enemy demolition, a total of 1535 miles of main line track will have to be relaid and 67,300 lineal feet of bridging must be reconstructed. Accomplishment of this work will require over 42,000 effective man months of labor, exclusive of supervisory and administrative personnel. Weight of the materiel and equipment to accomplish railway reconstruction amounts to 333,000 long tons, of which 74,000 long tons must be supplied from the U.S.

Reconstruction of road nets, particularly bridging, also presents special problems. By aerial photographs, ETOUSA has established the average length of bridge gap per mile of roads, and various intelligence sources were consulted to determine existing road construction. It has been determined that on the average for every mile of road there will be 13.9 lineal feet of bridging. Bridges of various lengths will occur in these percentages: 24% will be 10 to 30 ft gap; 34% will be 30 to 80 ft gap; 14,% 80 to 180 ft gap; and 28% over 180 ft. Of all this bridging, 90% on main supply routes will be destroyed and 75% on routes of lesser importance. Approximately 134 miles of road, which will be destroyed, will require reconstruction. Aside from reconstruction, a total of 6,100 miles of road will have to be maintained.

The total labor requirement for the maintenance and reconstruction of roads and bridging amounts to 1,548,000 man days, of which 1,282,000 will be military and 260,000 will be civilian.

15,800 long tons of asphalt will be required for road reconstruction and maintenance; 112,000 tons of road bridging will be required. This bridging will consist of 800 standard fixed Bailey sets (130 feet); 250 Standard Pontoon Bailey sets; 175 Heavy Increment Sets (Fixed) and 165 Heavy Pontoon Increment Sets. In addition to this material, 11,700 long tons of construction equipment will be needed. The total tonnage of all this material which must be transported to the Continent amounts to 139,500 long tons, of which 114,000 must be shipped from the U.S.

PART I: OUTLINE OF OPERATION OVERLORD
Tab 2e POL DISTRIBUTION PROBLEM

1. POL SUPPLY PROGRAM

The significant points in the POL supply plans are:

a. All supplies for the first 15 days will be packaged.

b. Bulk supplies of 80 Octane gasoline and Diesel fuel will be available by D+15.

c. Levels of supply and operating levels will be carried 40% in packages and 60% in bulk.

d. All daily consumption after D+15 will be supplied in bulk.

e. Storage of the level of supply will be 50% at ports and 50% at inland depots.

2. DISTRIBUTION IN PACKAGES

POL supplies in packages for motor transportation are stored in 14 QM POL depots in the UK. Approximately 250,000 gross tons of POL are in storage in reserve. During the first 41 days of the operation 165,000 gross tons will be required; of this total approximately 91,000 tons will be required in packages. It is expected that bulk POL will be available by D+15.

The peak movement to ports occurs during the first 14 days when all replacement and build up of levels will be entirely in packages. The peak is estimated to represent 1350 wagon trains (total 392 tons per train). All 14 QM POL depots will participate in the movement of POL supplies until about D+41, and after that movement will be confined to 4 depots at a time. Until D+41, 14 Gasoline Supply Companies will be retained in UK. The number will decrease progressively until only 4 will required by D+90. It is believed that all transportation between depots and railheads can be furnished by the organic transportation of Gasoline Supply Companies.

Preloading of coasters with packages will be required for assault and follow-up requirements, a portion to be skid-loaded.

Bulk shipments will be made in small tankers from a south coast port to one major and one minor port on the Continent, and possibly to one additional minor port.

During the period D to D+41, 9 QM POL depots will be established on the Continent, located with due regard to ports, pipeline, and distribution requirements. These depots will be in the hands of Gasoline

Supply Companies. Three QM Petroleum Testing Laboratories will be in operation at this time.

Regardless of availability of bulk POL, a supply of packages will flow continuously to the Continent to build up the can population and to replace lost cans. Lubricants will be continuously handled in packages. By D+41, approximately 1,500,000 cans, in addition to T/E cans on vehicles, will be in depots. 11,500,000 cans will have been stockpiled in QM POL depots in UK on D-Day.

3. BULK POL

Gasoline consumption during the period from D to D+90 is estimated to require approximately 5,000 tons per day at D+20, rising to a requirement for approximately 10,500 tons per day by D+90. By D+14, seven days of supply for Field Forces and 14 days of supply for Air Forces will have been established. By D+41, the figures are 14 and 21 days, respectively. Consumption is expected to be 10% in and around port areas, 30% along the lines of communication, and 60% in the forward areas. Aviation gasoline will be delivered to within 40 miles of Air Force installations.

Pipeline and storage tanks will be placed at or near QM depots, or in locations accepted and coordinated with the Quartermaster. Tanks up to D+41 will not exceed 800 tons. 850 miles of 6" pipeline, 460 miles of 4" pipeline, and 100,000 tons capacity of bolted steel will be required.

The program will require 10 Engineer Petroleum Distribution Companies and 1 General Service Regiment for assistance in pipeline construction, in addition to the QM Gasoline Supply Companies previously mentioned. Approximately 37,400 long tons of equipment will be consumed in installing the bulk POL system.

PART I: OUTLINE OF OPERATION OVERLORD
TAB 2f: CIVIL AFFAIRS PROBLEM

1. CIVIL AFFAIRS OBJECTIVE

The primary objective of Civil Affairs operations is the effective control of the civilian population to prevent its interference with military operations and to make the maximum use of local resources for the benefit of these operations. A corollary of this objective is the maintenance of certain minimum supplies to the civilian population, to establish adequate standards of public health and to prevent the civil population from becoming a burden upon the military. The standard established by the Combined Chiefs of Staff for foodstuffs is an average ration of 2000 calories per person per day, plus such medical, sanitary and clothing supplies as may be necessary. Of these supplies, the maximum amounts are to be obtained from indigenous resources, and only the deficiency is to be provided from stocks under military control.

While it is considered that army participation in rehabilitation work or in handling Civil Affairs supplies will not normally extent *[sic]* beyond the area of military operations, the attainment of the objective given above, however, may necessitate an extension of army responsibilities.

This is possible under conditions of forced invasion, as the lateral limits of the military area may have to be extended to take over ports, or other rail or communication facilities, in order to provide necessary additional means for supply movements to support the operation. This contingency seems particularly applicable in the case of a collapse condition on the Continent. The President in his letter to the Secretary of War, dated 10 November 1943, raised this point and stated in effect that the plans of the military for the provision of relief under collapse conditions should embrace the entire civilian population for the area of N. W. Europe.

2. <u>CLASSES OF SUPPLY</u>

Civil Affairs supplies fall into four general classes, as follows:

<u>a</u>. <u>Items necessary for immediate relief, consisting of</u>: Food, clothing, medical and sanitary supplies.

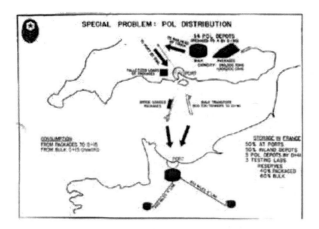

b. Items necessary for distribution of relief, consisting of: Emergency feeding equipment, fuel and initial repairs to public utility, communication, and transportation systems.

c. Items required to re-establish production of natural resources, such as coal, oil, etc., for military or civilian use.

d. Items which will have the effect of reducing the direct relief burden at the earliest possible date, consisting of: agriculture implements and seeds, raw material for rehabilitation of the textile industry.

In general, items under a. b. and c. will be included within military responsibility under conditions of either forced invasion or collapse conditions. Items under d. may only be included under collapse conditions, as military responsibility has been generally limited to a "yardstick" period of six months from the opening of operations in any area; and the handling of this class of supplies in a strictly forced operational condition, has to be further considered in the light of what the military can bring into any given area with existing shipping and transportation limitations.

3. ESTIMATED TONNAGES REQUIRED (US ZONE) BY GENERAL CLASSIFICATION, FOR FORCED (a) OCCUPATIONAL OPERATIONS, OR FOR (b) COLLAPSE CONDITIONS.

a. Forced occupational operations, from date of invasion to date; plus 120 days:

Food	116,260 long tons
Clothing and blankets	5,224 long tons
Soap	3,489 long tons
Medical and sanitary supplies	1,257 long tons
Ethel and lubricants	15,114 long tons
Emergency feeding equipment	337 long tons
TOTAL	141,681 long tons

The above are only estimated civilian requirements compiled by SHAEF for the first four months of the operation. They include consideration of the population within the area within time limits given that will require assistance, and that will be uncovered as the operation progresses. Further requirements will be compiled upon the basis of estimates from the field, taking into consideration bulk civilian supplies found available, the capacity of any given area to feed its people, and other rehabilitation requirements, as dictated by military necessity and local conditions.

b. Estimated requirements - collapse conditions (US Zone) for six months:

Food	520,665 long tons
Medical and sanitary supplies	2,599 long tons
Soap	18,741 long tons
Fuel and lubricants	375,995 long tons
Clothing and blankets	13,263 long tons
Clothing for military labor	317 long tons
Industrial first aid equipment	7,650 long tons
Emergency feeding equipment.	408 long tons
TOTAL	939,638 long tons

The tonnages and items given above may have to be further increased as the scope of military supply responsibility may be increased.

4. It is desired to emphasize that the above are estimates only, and that in either event the figures given may be materially altered by conditions affected by enemy armies. That is as to whether the area remains "unscorched", or is progressively destroyed ("scorched") as the enemy retreats.

5. As indicted it the tonnage figures stated above, which have to supplement normal military supply requirements, the responsibility of civilian supply is the major problem presented in carrying out the given objective of Civil Affairs Operations.

6. The carrying out of the objective may be further complicated or increased by a considerable refugee problem. From recent available information on the number of displaced persons in Western Europe, it is estimated that there are:

   *3,500,000 displaced persons in France

     450,000 displaced persons in Belgium

   1,125,000 displaced persons in Holland

   8,000,000 displaced persons in Germany

NOTE: * Estimates by COSSAC, 5 November 1943.

These consist of European Nationals, including Todt Workers, Civil Prisoners, Evacuees, Refugees, Enemy Armed Forces, and Prisoners of War. These may start a vast homeward movement that in order to control, to keep our military lines of communication open and prevent interference with military operations, may involve Civil Affairs provision of additional refugee shelter enclosures and enlarged emergency feeding centers.*

NOTE: * It is desired to add one additional statement to the above memorandum, i.e. that practically the entire Civil Affairs supply requirements for US Zone under forced occupational operations have been made available in the UK, and that approximately 250,000 tons of civilian supplies under collapse conditions have been made available in the UK for the US Zone.

PART I: <u>OUTLINE OF OPERATION OVERLORD</u>
TAB 3: <u>DEVELOPMENT OF COMMUNICATIONS ZONE</u>

1. The Communications Zone will develop from the beach areas initially assaulted and will be enlarged with the forward movement of the Field Forces. The beach areas will be under the command, initially, of the Commanding General, First Army. The personnel and equipment needed for the operation of beach areas will be provided by the First Army, with such additional SOS units attached as may be necessary. It is expected that when operation over beaches ceases, the beach units, less SOS units attached, will be assigned to Army Group Reserve for similar use elsewhere, or to US Armies for general use. The attached SOS units will be available to the Advance Section for duty.

During the initial period, the Army Service Area will include the beaches. SOS personnel allotted to the First Army for operation of rear installations will eventually be under the control of the Advance Section. Such SOS personnel will revert to control of Advance Section upon establishment of any Army rear boundary.

The boundary between U.S. and British forces will be the line Port-en-Bessin, River Drome from Escures, thence road Age - St. Paul du Vernay, Livry, Cahagnes, Jurques (all inclusive to British forces).

When an army rear boundary is designated, a Communication Zone will be established which will include all ports and beaches in operation at that time. The Communications Zone will be established about D+20 and will be under command of C-in-C, 21st Army Group, until such time as the First U.S. Army Group is designed to command in the U.S. Sector.

There has already been activated in England, a Hq Advance Section which will operate the Advance Section throughout OVERLORD. After reorganization and absorbing SOS units, which from D to about D+20 will be with First Army, the Advance Base Section will be assigned maintenance areas directly supporting the Combat Zone as long as lateral limits or other circumstances permit. Troops of the Advance Section operating fixed installations in the Communication Zone will not move forward with Advance Section, but will be replaced by new units as the need arises in forward areas.

The maintenance of necessary records, stock control of supplies and equipment, port development and operation, signal communications, construction and operation of railroads, control and operation of motor transport, and command of all Communications Zone troops is the responsibility of Hq Advance Section until Hq Communications Zone becomes operational.

In addition to the Advance Section, the Communication Zone will be comprised of two Base Sections, to be called Base Sections One and Two. Coincident with the capture of the Loire ports soon after D+40, Hq Base Section One, which will have been organized and held in readiness in UK until called forward, will undertake the rehabilitation and operation of these ports. Shortly thereafter, it will develop the Brittany peninsula as a principal supply base in support of offensive operations in northeast France.

On arrival of Base Section One, Hq Forward Echelon, Communications Zone will become operational and will assume command of the entire Communications Zone. Forward Echelon, Communications Zone will be responsible for maintenance of stock records of supplies and equipment, construction, operation and control of lines of communication.

In the progress of the operation, displacement of the Advance Section will be necessitated to enable it to continue direct support of the advancing combat elements. So that, soon after D+50, Hq Base Section Two, organized and held in readiness in the United Kingdom, will be called forward and will undertake command and operation of the Continental area relinquished by Advance Section.

The development of lines of communication in OVERLORD is interesting, in that their direction will change on about D+40 from North-South along the axis Cherbourg-Virte to a general East-West direction along the axis Brest-Laval. The reason for this change is threefold; primarily to fit into the tactical plan; also, the progressive development of beaches and ports; and finally, storage considerations.

Initially and until about D+40, the flow of supplies will come over the beaches and through the ports of the Cherbourg peninsula South to using combat units. A general storage area located East of Granville and

North of St. Hilaire will be organized during this period to accommodate reserve supply build-up.

After D+40, the Brittany ports will be opened up during the period when the perimeter of the Brittany peninsula is allocated to the Communications Zone. The flow of supplies then will be generally East to the using units.

During the period D+70 to D+90, and beyond, a general storage area roughly bounded by Rennes-Virte-Laval-Secre-Chateaubriand will be organized to accommodate reserve build-up.

By D+90, there will be over 1,200,000 US troops and about 250,000 US vehicles on the Continent of Europe. The problem of providing all that will be needed by the forward Air Force, Infantry, Tank, Artillery and other combat elements will be staggering even under the best conceivable conditions for OVERLORD. The only way to simplify these problems and to support adequately the operation is to lay down in the Theater everything that can now with reason be expected to be required.

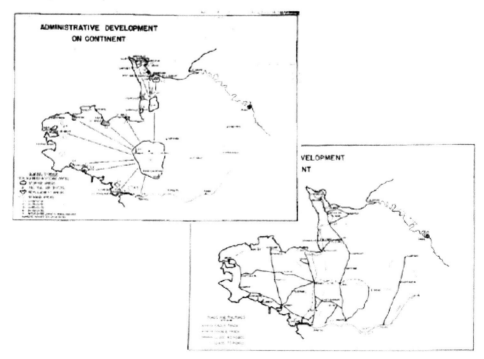

CPSIA information can be obtained at www.ICGtesting.com
Printed in the USA
LVOW13s0051061213

364054LV00001B/1/P